Sage Advice from Uncle Oscar

Boyhood Memories of Blue Hill

by **Sage Collins**

ISBN: 978-0-941238-20-5
LCCN: 2015955584

For Penobscot Books:
Caroline Spear, Editor
Jeremiah Savage, Cover Design, Book Design, Layout
Tevlin Schuetz, Foreword, Author Photos, Cape Racer Sled Photo

Photographs in the text are from the 1961-1965 files
of *The Weekly Packet*, a weekly newspaper published
in Blue Hill, Maine, by Penobscot Bay Press, Inc.
weeklypacket.com

Cover Image: "Cape Racers," pen and ink, by Leslie Moore, 2008.
First published in The Brooksville Breeze newsletter in 2008; used
with permission. Leslie Moore is a pen-and-ink artist and woodblock
printmaker in Belfast, Maine, whose first love is drawing pets.
Find her PenPets website at *PenPets.com*.

Published by

Penobscot Books
a division of Penobscot Bay Press Community Information Services
P.O. Box 36, 69 Main Street, Stonington, Maine 04681 USA
Tel: 207-367-2200
Email: books@pbp.me
Web: penbaypress.me
Printed in the USA by 360 Digital Books, Kalamazoo, Michigan USA

I dedicate this book to my grandparents, James and Margaret Billings—"Bamp" and "Marnie." Without them in my life, the childhood that I experienced would not have been possible.

And to my wife, Alexa, who encouraged me in this endeavor and whose sense of balance and composition was indispensable to the final product.

Table of Contents

Foreword

Forget food, water and shelter; memories are the most important thing to any person.

As individuals, we rely completely on our memories for all we know: from basic survival skills (eating, tying our shoelaces...the important stuff), to our beliefs and strongest convictions, to our very identities. Socially, memories cement our relationships with family and friends, our senses of place and community, history and culture itself.

And memories are funny things. Sometimes we swear they're real when they're not, and if we're left alone with memories long enough we can really fool ourselves with them (Politicianfolk occasionally claim to "misspeak." Will they soon grant themselves the latitude to misremember?).

But sharing memories is a mixed bag, too, because there is always opportunity for two or more people to disagree. As individuals, our recollections are tempered by our own perspectives, of course, so when looking back, memories shared must usually be arrived at through consensus (sometimes driven by the loudest or most persistent voice).

And memories are fragile things. They can die. When this happens, reality becomes just a little less concrete and a little more questionable—even suspect. There are things we'd like to forget, of course, but when we lose our grasp on memories, we lose portions of our lives. When we lose whole swaths of memories, we begin to lose ourselves, and who are we then?

Enter the storyteller. While she or he entertains us with tales—some taller than others, certainly—storytellers can preserve memories and even fortify their presence in our minds. By including details beyond the main action of a story—like the effects of sunlight in a room, a sensation, the sound of the earth under foot when one runs, walks or shuffles, a scent in the air, or a sudden thought or observation, even extraneous to the matter at hand—storytellers can connect us with the humanness of their experiences. We find ourselves again, and the people, places and moments described become meaningful to us, even a part of us.

We are continually moving ahead in time, on a sort of ride we can never exit. And because all things change in time, the importance of storytelling cannot be overstated; it transcends the mere recording of events and becomes the closest thing to time travel we can experience.

Whether he means to be or not, Sage Collins is a time traveler, and he brings us along with him, too, much to our delight. Like all good storytellers, he carries us into the moment, and we finish the story in better spirits, with traces of the experience still lingering in our senses. Sage transports us to an earlier time in Blue Hill, Maine, the small coastal town where he spent his childhood. It's a place that has changed considerably over the years, like many similar communities along the coast. Blue Hill was a smaller place during Sage's youth. There were year-round people—the vast majority with long family histories in town—and then summer residents.

Sage explained how things were different for kids back then. "We were free range." If a child was not back by supper, parents figured he or she was eating somewhere else, at a friend's house or with other family members. Kids spent a lot of

time outside, too, and they learned by watching. "Parents never sat you down and told you stuff; you paid attention." A person's reputation meant a lot more in a town where everyone knew each other, and people usually "did the honorable thing," Sage says.

Nowadays more people live in the area, and many more of the year-round residents are "from away," Sage says; the time when a person knew or recognized everyone or at least some member of another's family is no more. While he could surely lament (as many people do) about how small-town coastal Maine has changed, Sage instead keeps his "Uncle Oscar's Beeline" stories pure, sharing the gifts of his recollections with readers indiscriminately and in good-humored fashion, thus keeping a memory—and more than that: a period in time— alive. Because he is recounting childhood experiences, we are treated to a perspective colored with all of the wonder felt by a boy learning about his world, in addition to his developing confidence and occasionally impish inclinations. As such, Sage may be as much a local historian as he is a storyteller. He is gratified by those who enjoy his columns, many of whom share a connection to the area and remember the way it was "in a time that has gone by," as Sage describes.

His interests were like those of any other Blue Hill youth during that era: He liked bikes, boats and being a kid. His stories consist of tales of occasional mischief; explorations of the exquisite qualities of peanut butter and Marshmallow Fluff sandwiches; "boy time," which passes at a much slower rate than that of other people, and more.

And what about Uncle Oscar? Well, he is Sage's muse: his great-uncle, Oscar Billings. Oscar himself was larger-than-life in a way, and not only to Sage but to other family members, too. A generally quiet man, Oscar had mercurial moments when he would spring into animation. But Oscar is largely an archetype in Sage's stories, representing male family members who have influenced Sage during his life. Oscar plays himself often enough, but he also plays Sage's maternal grandfather, Jim Billings Sr. and Sage's father, Waldo. Occasionally Oscar embodies Sage's uncle, Jim Billings Jr., as well as his paternal grandfather, Irving.

Sage's stories often finish with realizations of sorts. These are not morals per se, but larger truths can usually be found. And Sage says the stories contain no exaggerations; on the contrary, things often need to be toned down out of consideration for the audience—as well as to protect both the innocent and the guilty. Sage changes people's names occasionally to this end, if the shenanigans would cause embarrassment— and some participants are still around, too.

Born in Blue Hill in 1947, Sage grew up there during

the 1950s, and his family connection to the town goes back generations. His mother and father, Louise and Waldo, were also born in Blue Hill, as was his younger sister, Autumn. His paternal grandmother was born on Long Island in Blue Hill Bay, when a community still thrived there, and her father manned the island's mail boat.

Sage attended Blue Hill Consolidated School and George Stevens Academy before heading off to Southern Maine Technical Institute, where he studied electronics. He, along with most of his class, went to work for General Electric in Syracuse, New York, after graduation. Sage's number came up for the draft for Vietnam but was deferred. Soon after, he returned to Blue Hill, where he took up land surveying, a job he immediately enjoyed. "It's the best job in the world," Sage avows, due to its multifaceted nature involving math, cartography, history, archaeology, searching through deeds, knowledge of real estate law and many opportunities to help people. Being outdoors is a bonus, too, and being able to see a lot of the area—by invitation rather than trespassing—keeps Sage grounded.

Sage did not write outside of what was required by school assignments in his youth. He never scrawled dutifully in a diary, nor did he fashion poems for sweethearts. But he could definitely write, and English class was never a problem. " Give me an essay question, and I could fake it," Sage says. He may have inherited the knack; his father was published in *Downeast Magazine*, and an uncle on his paternal grandmother's side of the family was a painter, woodcarver and sometime poet.

In the late 1990s, Sage discovered his true passion for writing when he wrote a piece off the cuff for *Bearings*, a now defunct trade quarterly for surveyors in Maine. The magazine had called for story entries from its readership, and Sage's piece won the contest. The magazine's editor invited him to pen a regular column, and "Sage Advice from Uncle Oscar" began appearing in the publication. It was similar to "Uncle Oscar's Beeline" except that it most often dealt with surveying.

Sage wrote "Cape Racer Christmas," about his adventures with a Cape Racer sled, and this piece he sent to Publisher and Editor Nat Barrows at *The Weekly Packet*. Soon there were regular and semi-regular contributions, whenever Sage could finish stories and Nat could fit them on the paper's editorial page. *Sage Advice from Uncle Oscar* includes all the "Uncle Oscar's Beeline" columns published in *The Weekly Packet*, from the beginning in 2010 through 2014.

Sage still lives in Blue Hill, just up the hill from town, with his wife of 22 years, Alexa. He has two grown children; his daughter, Amber, her husband, John, and their two children live close-by in Cape Rosier, and his son, Josh, and his wife, Holly, recently moved back to Blue Hill.

Sage enjoys renovating and building houses, working outside, cutting wood, and occasional travel. He admits to dabbling in music as well: "I like to play guitar, but I'm no good at it."

—Tevlin Schuetz

Cape Racer Christmas

The Christmas tree went up shortly after Thanksgiving and was taken down on New Year's Day. It seemed that almost daily another present would mysteriously appear beneath its fragrant branches. Shaking presents was frowned upon by the adults, but my cousins (all girls) and I made frequent inventories of the loot. Every year there was one gift to Uncle Oscar that sloshed. I never saw Uncle Oscar take a drink, but each Christmas after we were finished picking the tree, he would retire, together with his unopened gift, to his room, not to emerge until the next morning.

On one particular Christmas I received two sleds. The first was of a new design, the second as old as history could be traced on the Maine coast. The former was called a "flying saucer." It was a disk made from aluminum. To operate this beast, one sat cross-legged, hands tightly gripping the handles while spinning wildly out of control down the hill. Devastation and destruction seemed imminent with each outing. What great fun!

The latter was a sled called a Cape Racer. I believe that its design was particular to this part of the coast, but variations may exist elsewhere. Some say that the Cape Racer originated in Cape Rosier, Brooksville, hence its name. One might now occasionally find a Cape Racer in an antique shop, but I know of no one today who builds these sleds. To my knowledge they were never mass-produced, each being built as needed and no two being exactly alike.

The design of a Cape Racer puts one in mind of a ladder. It was a long, narrow sled with full length runners often extending a short way out the back. This gave the sled a rakish air and added to its function. Its low runners were covered with flat steel and the closely spaced rungs were loosely fitted between the runners, the tension adjusted by a turnbuckle.

That fall Uncle Oscar had built a Cape Racer for me in his workshop. It was a short, kid-size version with oak runners and ash rungs. Uncle Oscar explained that he had used sleigh steel instead of soft flat steel for the runners. Sleigh steel was a hardened steel, used for the runners of sleighs, and was particularly slippery on snow and ice. He had painted the sled with many coats of red enamel. It was a real beauty.

Cape Racers had the reputation of being the "fastest sled known to man or God" and this reputation was not wholly undeserved, but the conditions had to be just right. The snow needed to be firmly packed, with thick crust or ice being the absolute best.

That year the weather did not cooperate. There was snow on the ground, but it was overcast and warm. Sunday afternoon found me in the field behind Cy Piper's barn. The field made a long hill, ending at the bottom with a patch of briars and a small brook. The sticky snow was great for snowballs but not for sliding. The Cape Racer was useless in this kind of snow so I concentrated on the flying saucer. Many successive trips down the hill yielded a packed tract of snow, concave to the curved shape of the flying saucer and ending in a ramp mounded from the wet snow, creating a sort of ski jump.

When I had finished the wind had backed to the nor'west and daylight was fading. The mercury fell with the coming darkness as I headed back to the house for supper.

The school day passed with the immeasurable slowness of youth, but finally the closing bell rang. Running from the bus I grabbed my new Cape Racer and headed for the hill. This was her maiden voyage, her shakedown cruise, and this run had been planned in my imagination all day, with every detail worked out in my mind.

The snow had frozen; the thick crust easily held my weight as I ran toward the end of the tract, now solid ice. A running jump, belly down on the sled found me flying down the hill. At first it was great, but the speed increased and continued to increase at an exponential rate. Feeling like a man who had jumped off a bridge and realizing partway into his fall that maybe this wasn't such a good idea, I knew that I was committed. About half way down the Cape Racer was approaching light speed. This realization became apparent due to the sensation of time slowing down. Hitting the ramp at the bottom lofted the Cape Racer and me towards the stratosphere. Up, up we went and, as in a dream, I watched the ground move slowly beneath us. From that altitude I saw the snow give way to the patch of briar brush and alders. Would I clear the brook? A moot point since death was the only oddment to my situation. In slow motion my sled and I descended and, after what seemed an eternity, we crashed just short of the brook but not quite clear of the briar patch. The Cape Racer folded beneath my weight and exploded into a hundred pieces. I remember thinking that it wasn't every day that one got to die, and that I should pay particular attention so that I would know what it was like.

I lay in the snowbank unable to move, wondering how long it would take for them to find my cold, frozen body.

A certain cosmic adjustment is necessary after one returns from a near light speed trip through hyperspace, and at first I was not quite certain as to whether or not I had actually died. Accordingly, as I found my feet, it seemed as though Heaven—or could this be Hell?—was very similar to winter in Maine. In later years, I believe that a Maine winter is a lot of both.

Gathering together what pieces of the sled I could find, I lugged the assortment back to the house. Remembering the feelings that were inside me then still strikes a chord in my heart. There was first the relief of being alive, coupled with the disappointment of losing my pristine, wonderful sled, and the fear of punishment for my carelessness in breaking my new present.

As it turned out, the most phenomenal thing about a Cape Racer is that it is virtually indestructible. What looked like a total loss turned out to be a simple matter of reassembling the pieces. Uncle Oscar had it back in form in no time flat and nothing was ever mentioned about my breaking the sled in the first place.

I had that sled for many years, but, as often happens, time slipped away and so did the Cape Racer. When Mom passed away some years back and we were cleaning out the place, I half expected to see it stuffed up in a rafter in the attic, but I never found it.

Sometimes, even now, when the snow is just right and the wind blows cold from the nor'west, I can still feel it at the end of the rope, dancing along behind me, ready for the next ride.

The Bee Tree

As readers know, "Uncle Oscar's Bee Line" has been a feature on the editorial page of *The Weekly Packet* for a number of years. My choice of the title was not random, but based on a real event that stands out in my memory like a plaid sport coat at the junior prom.

Snowflakes the size of silver dollars were decorating the post office parking lot. A March storm, overstaying its welcome like a ten-day house guest, was making a sloppy mess of Blue Hill village. In December, the fall of snow would have been welcomed by all, but by March most Mainers have seen enough snow and are ready for Spring.

"Good morning, Oscar. Great day to line bees."

"One of the best!" was my reply as I stomped the wet snow from my boots.

The lobby was crowded. A lady at the front of the line looked at the speakers questioningly and quickly went back to her purchase of postage stamps. Murray Tapley was the only one who ever called me Oscar and, though the joke was old, it still brought a chuckle to both of us.

Pulling out of the post office, the bright windows of the old home place caught my attention. Acting on impulse, I turned into the driveway and parked in the spot previously reserved for Uncle Oscar's Model A Ford. The falling snow added a certain surreal quality to the scene. The old house is now an architect's office and though Time had made some changes, she had thoughtfully left enough intact so that, with the snow to blur things a little, it was easy enough for me to see the summer of 1959 through the frosted windshield.

One of my chores was to mow the lawn, for which I was paid fifty cents. Though the money was good, the work usually occupied most of my Saturday. The front lawn facing Main Street was steep and terraced and was a bear to mow. Hearing me complain, Uncle Jimmy told me that I was lucky to have a power mower. "Back when I was a boy," he continued, "I had to mow that lawn with a push mower." Knowing that fact didn't do a thing to make me feel any better about the prospect as I continued to pull on the cord in a futile effort to start the nefarious device. At length, I took a break from pulling at the Briggs & Stratton devil in order to catch my breath.

There was a patch of clover blossoms on the back lawn that I had strict instructions not to mow. It was in this patch of clover that Uncle Oscar held sway on afternoons when the weather proved clement. An ancient maple thoughtfully provide a dappled shade and the cool breezes off the inner bay tempered the late August sunshine. That afternoon found Uncle Oscar sitting under the maple in the green Adirondack chair that had been placed there for his sole use.

Even from a distance it was plain that Uncle Oscar had set out his bee-lining paraphernalia on the flat arm of the Adirondack. At that time it was a sport to line bees in order to discover the location of a wild beehive. An informal competition developed among the old timers who practiced lining bees and it became a point of honor and pride in finding and eventually harvesting a wild bee tree.

As I remember, the bee tree belonged not to the landowner on whose property it grew, but to the person who found it.

19

If one were fortunate enough to find a bee tree, it would be necessary to "mark" or brand it in such a way to stake a claim. Initials were carved in the trunk or a shirt or jacket could be tied to a limb. That claim was then honored by any subsequent finder. Uncle Oscar was the best, and many a late autumn would find the kitchen counter overflowing with tubs and buckets of wild comb honey.

A couple more tugs on the lawn mower produced no results, save for a slight cramp in my arm. If only I had that push mower that Uncle Jimmy had spoken so highly of, the lawn would have been mowed by now.

Uncle Oscar hadn't shifted his position for the last five minutes. He sat bolt upright, hands gripping the arms of the Adirondack, and his steel eyes stared straight ahead. The only movement was the wind through his mane of white hair.

Something had been bothering Uncle Oscar for the past week and today it seemed to have come to a head. Uncle Oscar was a quiet man. I had never seen him angry, but there was the underlying sense that I probably never wanted to.

The distance between the lawnmower and the Adirondack was about thirty yards. Across that short space, beneath a cloudless sky, there came suddenly the sensation of something akin to an imminent lightning strike.

The moment was broken in an instant. Uncle Oscar was striding purposefully toward his Model A. The young boy by the lawnmower arrested his attention and he paused and looked in my direction. "Want to go for a ride?"

"Sure, where are we going?" Not that it mattered, any excuse not to mow the lawn.

"Just checking on a bee tree."

Epiphany was a word that had not yet entered my young vocabulary, but, in hindsight, it nailed it. Standing alone in the late afternoon sun, surrounded by the equally bewildered honeybees, I could make no sense of it all. The old maple tree lay in pieces, its honey gone. Uncle Oscar's jacket, his "claim," still wrapped around an ax-hewn limb, lay within plain sight. The remains of the smudge that had been built to smoke out the bees were barely cold. Remembering the half eaten Red Sails candy bar that continued to melt in my shirt pocket provided the answer. Chocolate has been scientifically proven to rejuvenate the gray matter and it was the work of a moment to remove the paper wrapper and pop the delicious confection into my mouth. Experience told me that the wrapper still had some good in it. It was a messy job to get all the remaining chocolate off but, in life, good things are often messy.

Suddenly, like the final chapter of an Agatha Christie mystery, the scales fell from my eyes and the pieces all fell into place.

As you may remember, Uncle Oscar spent many a summer lining bees from the comfort of an Adirondack chair located in a patch of clover blossoms. A competition resulted among the old timers as to who could line a honey bee back to its wild hive, the bee tree. The result was that the finder marked the tree and anyone who subsequently found that tree would honor the other's claim. In the late fall the honey was harvested and my grandmother's biscuits took on the quality of ambrosia.

Uncle Oscar's demeanor had changed of late. The bees from his bee tree had not been visiting his treacle, or sugar water, and he knew what had happened. The remains of the bee tree confirmed his suspicions. Someone had taken it, and he knew who.

The race of the Model A's engine brought me out of my reverie. Covering the distance back to the woods road in near record time I slid into the passenger's seat. It would have been quicker except the laces on one of my Red Ball Keds tripped me up in the home stretch. The atmosphere in the cab was electrified and not a little frightening. Uncle Oscar was rightfully angry, and it was clear that a drama in the world of men was about to unfold.

The Model A's afterburners cut in immediately after takeoff and we were airborne. The once bumpy woods road became as smooth as a tarred highway as we skipped along, occasionally making ground contact just long enough to rocket the Model A back into the stratosphere. The gravel of the Back Road barely felt the weight of our tires, and upon reaching the tar Uncle Oscar deviated from his preference for second gear and coaxed the Model A into overdrive. The engine screamed a little in protest but soon came around to the spirit of the moment. We were flying. Henry Ford would have been proud had he been along for the ride.

Just where we stopped I will not say. I suspect that I am the sole remaining party who knows the particulars. After a fashion we came to earth in a barnyard. A man who looked to be about the same vintage as Uncle Oscar was next to the henhouse, splitting wood, maple. He turned and faced us. It was a time when everybody knew everybody and I recognized him immediately.

"You stay right here! Don't you dare get out of this car!"

The steam from the radiator partially obscured my view as Uncle Oscar crossed to where the man was standing. At that time men took care of matters such as this between themselves. Strong words were exchanged and the two repaired out of sight and earshot behind the barn.

Time is not always linear when the fabric of a place is rent, so there is no way of knowing how long the "conversation" lasted. Sitting in the front seat, not daring to move, I pondered the wellbeing of the man by the woodpile.

The note of the engine, like the mood of the occupants, was more subdued on the ride back home. Uncle Oscar was quiet as he switched off the Model A's engine and went into the house. The lawnmower was waiting just where I had left it and to my dismay it started on the first pull.

The following morning I went out on the piazza and there, next to the old front door, were two washtubs full of wild honey. Uncle Oscar appeared behind me, his face bearing only the slightest trace of a smile. One man's honor had been preserved and another man's rightful honey had been restored.

For years I never fully understood my purpose in this adventure, but the other day, while munching a Dove candy bar, in an epiphany, it came to me.

Time Is On My Side

Those who know the author will no doubt tell you that brevity is not his strongest suit. To him, "cutting a long story short" may require the better part of a Sunday afternoon.

My daughter tells me that every week when *The Weekly Packet* arrives, my grandchildren check to see if Bamp has a column. As Fate would have it, Elana and John were at the house and the latest edition was on the table. They found the column and, as a treat, I offered to read it to them. It went along smoothly at first, but mid-way into the meat of the story a slight restlessness was noted in the audience. By the three-quarter mark, the restlessness had turned to a polite resignation. Time started to drag, and instead of a *Packet* column, it felt like I was reading the unabridged works of James Michener. Without saying a word, my new editors were on the job. Let's see if it works.

"Time is on my side, yes, it is..."—the truck radio and the engine both coming to life together in the cool early morning Blue Hill air. With last night's dreams quietly evaporating back into the subconscious, the year was once again 1964. Sitting in my '56 Chevy, savoring the freedom that comes but once in a young man's life, long-forgotten memories came flooding back, memories as delicious as Aunt Helen's birthday cake. Driving down the camp road, the radio stayed in 1964 with Chuck Berry's "No Particular Place To Go" pounding through the dashboard speaker. The gravel giving way to the pavement of the main road, the old Chevy straining under a heavy foot, leaving a trail of blue exhaust smoke, with a clear sky, a half tank of gas and a two-gallon can of Sapphire Motor Oil in the trunk, a summer day of limitless possibilities was mine.

Up ahead a flagman is waving me to a stop. As if on cue, Chuck Berry gives way to Chad and Jeremy's "Yesterday's Gone." The spell is broken—2010 returns.

Perhaps in 1964 both Mick Jagger and I believed that time was indeed on our side. I can't speak for Mick but, of late, doubts are beginning to creep in.

Albert Einstein said of time that the distinction between past, present and future is only a stubbornly persistent illusion. He also had a theory of relativity, which has time slowing down as speed is increased. This is all very well, but what Professor Einstein should have addressed is the far more practical matter as to why time passes faster as we get older. An informal poll made by the author re this phenomenon reveals that this is a generally recognized truth. If time is an illusion, as Einstein contends, it's a darn good one.

Duane Gray remarked that it seemed like only yesterday that he and I were sitting on the TA-CO steps sharing an order of Ted Horton's french fries. As an aside said with no fear of rebuke, the afore-mentioned french fries were, without doubt, the best in the country, if not the world. Their equal will never be seen again while we are on this side of the grass.

My personal time theory, though it has fewer calculations than Einstein's, is borne of experiential rather than of empirical knowledge. My theory holds that "youth time" is roughly equivalent to "dog time." The factor of seven seems about right. Cast your memory back. Remember a day in the fifth grade classroom for example. Every hour that passed seemed like seven. Summer vacations stretched out seemingly forever, and it took decades to reach the age of 17, old enough to get a driver's license.

We all seem to have a need to know what time it is. Growing up, a new Timex watch—"It takes a licking and keeps on ticking"—could be had for about seven dollars and if one ever broke you could send it back to the factory with fifty cents, plus postage, and a few months later a new watch, sort of like the one you sent, would appear in your mailbox. I went through any number of Timex watches, waterproof, shockproof, dust resistant, fluorescent numbers that glowed in the dark, everything a boy could want. Most of them even kept fairly good time.

A.B. Herrick, who owned a large construction business at the location of Blue Hill's EBS store, sometimes saw fit to hire me as summer help. B. was a man who was very particular about time. The dinner break, noon, was exactly 30 minutes long, from 11 to 11:30. If B. were on the job site, 11:28 would find him pulling his watch from his pocket and flipping open the cover. "By thunder, boys, time to be getting back to work." And you can bet we did.

Uncle Oscar also carried a pocket watch. His was unusual in that it had only two hands. You may think that having two hands is not a unique feature for a watch, but the two hands to which I refer were the second hand, which he used exclusively for lining bees, and the hour hand. The minute hand on Uncle Oscar's pocket watch was permanently missing.

Uncle Oscar got along just fine with a watch that had only an hour hand. His day was structured more by nature and the seasons than by the clock. Perhaps time was on his side.

32 Special

Oscar was the oldest in the family and with age came a certain responsibility.

His father, my great-grandfather, had marched with Sherman and at the end of the Civil War had ended up somewhere in Georgia. Great-grandfather had started out the march in Ohio or Illinois, but upon his return trip home he headed toward the Nor'east and kept going until he fetched up in Blue Hill.

Oscar had spent a part of the fall season in the "County" picking potatoes. Even back then the potatoes were somehow dug mechanically, if using a team and some sort of excavating device constituted mechanically. My experience with potatoes was that they were dug with a clam hoe. But, however they were dug, they needed to be picked up and separated from the like-colored stones and Maine dirt that gave them nourishment.

Picking potatoes amounted to a good deal of back-bending labor. Like raking blueberries, it was not an hourly job. How many George Washingtons you put in your pocket at the end of a week's labor was directly proportional to the number of potatoes you put in the barrel.

Flush with cash, Oscar stopped overnight in the Queen City. It was fall and a long winter lay ahead. Exhilarated by the sights of a big city and lofted by a hearty breakfast, he paused outside a storefront on Central Street. There in the shop window was a new Winchester Model 94, 32 Special. The year was 1902 and though the Model 94 Winchester had been out for a few years, the new 32 special was indeed "special." Uncle Oscar stepped inside, took the rifle from its place in the window and laid it on the counter. The old storekeeper eyed the boy with a questioning look and was about to send him off with the aid of the broom he was holding when Oscar added, "And ten boxes of shells."

The storekeeper collected the cartridges from the back shelf and returned to find Oscar, cash in hand.

The purchase of the deer rifle was an investment long overdue, assuring ample food for the family through the coming winter and many winters to come.

It was not too long ago when it was hard to be lazy and live in Maine. It was possible, perhaps even probable, that a lazy man could both starve to death and freeze to death simultaneously.

Back then an old person or a widow with children never wanted for food or firewood. The church and the community took care of their own. But a lazy man was in for some tough sledding.

That is not to say that some did not try to get by without working. Take Odlaw, for instance. Not that he considered himself lazy, simply blessed with a lack of ambition.

He had possessed a certain amount of responsibility when he was young and there was a family to be taken care of. However, in later years he had figured out that his wife, rather than eat poverty stew in a cold kitchen and endure the deprivations of self-inflicted indigence would get a job. This was a situation that greatly pleased Odlaw.

It finally reached a point in mid-December 1902 that reason returned to Hattie's throne and she returned to her family in Boston, leaving Odlaw to fend for himself.

Oscar heard of Odlaw's plight and on a Monday morning, straddling Christmas and New Year's, donned his beavertail snowshoes and walked the mile to Odlaw's place.

Odlaw was in his kitchen and seemed pleased to see Oscar. A chopping block was next to the table and a small, snow-covered getchel birch, limbs and all, was dragged across the floor. It was cold in the kitchen since the birch tree kept the outside door from closing and what little bit of it Odlaw had cut was refusing to burn in the cookstove.

Odlaw said that there were some potatoes down cellar and perhaps later on he would have another go at building a fire. "A lot of work in a fire, you know."

Oscar asked whether Odlaw had any meat to go with the potatoes. Odlaw's answer in the negative did not come as a surprise. Hunting season had passed and the law was back on deer. The law never stopped an honest man when he was hungry. A nearby deer yard was in a place well-known to both men and it would have been the work of a moment for Oscar to return with fresh meat, build a fire in Odlaw's stove and cook supper. Instead, Oscar provided the wherewithal for Odlaw to help himself. Oscar laid a box of cartridges on the table and stood his new 32 Special in the corner by the door, wishing Odlaw luck and saying he would be back later that week.

On New Year's morning Oscar stopped by to pick up his gun. Half of him expected to see a deer hanging in the barn; the other half was not surprised when he did not.

The Winchester was still standing in the corner and the box of shells lay unopened on the table. Stepping over the birch tree lying on the kitchen floor, Oscar stopped short in disbelief.

29

Next to a cheery fire sat Odlaw, eating a breakfast of ham and eggs.

"The ladies from the grange stopped by with this nice breakfast and Deacon Clough brought up a load of firewood. He even built the fire. 'Happy New Year,' he said."

Oscar put the box of cartridges in his coat pocket and collected the rifle from the corner.

Closing the door behind him, Oscar smiled and said, "Happy New Year, Odlaw."

Jump Start

A few years ago, as a Christmas gift, my wife had a remote starter installed on my pickup truck. I could say that she was tired of going out in the snow every morning to start my truck for me, but my policy is to keep these columns based in truth. These remote starter devices offered a certain luxury on a cold morning that was heretofore unheard of. One had to remember to set all the controls in the truck when parking it the night before—temperature and defroster on high and wipers off. Running the wipers when they were frozen down was not advised.

In the not-too-distant past the idea of a remote starter would have been laughable. Sure, they may have worked in the summer, but when the mercury hovered around zero there was just no way. Any morning when the overnight temperature dipped to zero, a good half of the cars in town would not start. At 15° below, nine out of ten cars, when the key was turned, would utter forth a sound like a dying duck, click a few times and lapse into silence.

One of the first things one learned about a car was how to start it. Each car had its own personality and the method of getting the motor started varied from vehicle to vehicle. It was wisdom gained by trial and error. One practiced throughout the summer and into fall until the inevitable morning of the test arrived.

It is still dark and the kitchen floor is cold as you stir up the embers in the stove and put in a couple of sticks of wood. Switching on the porch light confirms your fears. The thermometer in the window reads 2° below and there is a brisk wind kicking up snow devils in the driveway. What are the odds the old girl will start? Only one way to find out.

Pulling on your boots and taking your coat from a hook in the entry, you make your way into the dark driveway and pound on the frozen chrome door handle until the driver's door finally opens with groan. The key is in the switch. (It doesn't get lost if you always leave it there.) Settling in behind the wheel you remain silent for a respectable period of time before you attempt anything drastic. Your left foot pushes the clutch pedal to the floor and you pull the gearshift lever into neutral. It moves slowly, like a mixing spoon through heavy, frozen cake batter. Still holding the clutch pedal to the floor, you press the accelerator three times in quick secession, count to five, and turn the key. The engine turns over, sputters and quits. "Now, Tinkerbelle," (people often named their cars just so they could offer encouragement at such times) "I know you can do it!"

Count to five, hold the accelerator down and turn the key again. This time the engine catches twice before it stalls. Patience. You have only one more chance before the battery dies.

Tinkerbelle receives more words of encouragement, and the moment of truth has arrived. Resist the urge: don't touch the accelerator pedal. With the final turning of the key, a silent prayer to Oldsmobile, the patron saint of automobiles, wings its way heavenward.

The engine reluctantly turns over with all the drama of a B-movie and finally rumbles to life. Your right foot performs a subtle Goldilocks ballet on the gas pedal. Too much gas and the

engine will stall; too little will produce the same result.

After a fashion, Tinkerbelle reaches a point where she will run on her own and you leave her to warm up. Before returning to the kitchen to warm yourself up with a cup of coffee you break loose a stick of wood from the wood pile and put it behind the tire. Just to be on the safe side.

The term "jump start" has come to mean connecting cables between the batteries in two vehicles in order to start the one with a flat battery, but the origin of the term is somewhat different.

Our neighbor, Bert, owned a '52 Plymouth sedan. Plymouths of that era had a reputation for being nearly impossible to start in cold weather and Bert's was no exception. Wilbur worked for the town and, seeing Bert's situation, stopped to offer assistance. A stout chain was hooked from the back of Wilbur's Studebaker dump truck to the front bumper of the Plymouth. With Bert at the helm of the Plymouth, Wilbur pulled ahead and put a little tension on the chain. The tires on the Plymouth broke their icy moorings and the parade headed down the road. The idea was that, when "starting velocity" was attained, Bert would let the clutch out, the car would jump and usually start. Etiquette required that Bert blow his horn as soon as the car started. The parade continued down Main Street, through the village and out the East Blue Hill Road. At the top of Sand Hill, Wilbur looked in his rearview mirror and noticed exhaust from Bert's Plymouth. Wilbur stopped and unhooked the chain. "Sure took a while to get her started."

"Not too bad, just past the post office."

"What! Why didn't you blow your horn? I've towed you half way to Surry."

"I just wanted to let her warm up a mite."

Deep Breakfast

Uncle Oscar was always the first one up in the morning. He always stuck to the summer schedule, when it was daylight at 4:30 a.m. His regimen was not unique—Mainers are known to rise at an early hour, though there are exceptions. Sometimes, on Sundays, I find myself still beneath the counterpane until nearly 6.

The phrase "wake up and smell the coffee" has a special place in a far corner of my memory. Sometimes just the aroma of coffee brewing will transport me back in time to a February morning, Uncle Oscar and me in the kitchen, the crackling wood fire in the parlor stove the only sound breaking the morning's silence. Breakfast was a simple meal, varying little. Bacon and eggs were a staple, with yeast bread toasted on top of the kitchen stove. For those unfamiliar with this practice, it is quite simple. Sliced bread is placed on top of the stovelid; it toasts and is turned over. When both sides are done, it is removed and buttered. The taste cannot be duplicated by a modern electric toaster; there is nothing quite like it.

At that time, almost everyone kept chickens, mostly for the eggs, but sometimes for Sunday dinner. The chicken house was located out back, midway between the barn and the shop. Along with the chickens there was always a rooster. Roosters are mean, scary, protective beasts by nature and if one spied you within his domain he would make rooster noises and, if further provoked, fly at your face, feet first. Uncle Oscar would meet the Campine devil with a wave of his arm and send him flying.

It was not that easy for me when I gathered the breakfast eggs. A boy's imagination often came into play. The chicken house was the castle vault, the eggs were the jewels, the rooster a palace guard, and I, a master burglar. I was never sure what part the chickens themselves played in this fantasy. My personal opinion is that chickens are not the most intelligent of animals, and many a burglary was foiled by their unwarranted clucking, which alerted the rooster, I mean "palace guard," to the presence of an intruder. At such times, the experienced burglar swaps time for distance, and legs it to the safety of the woodshed, I mean his "secret hideout."

Ham and bacon were usually of the native variety. There were people who specialized in smoking hams and curing bacon. Newt Grindle, who lived on the East Blue Hill Road, was an expert. It would be difficult to find anyone who had sampled Newt's efforts who would bestow anything but the highest praise. Not an authority on the subject myself, it is my understanding that the secret is in the "pickle" and Newt's recipe for pickle no doubt followed him to the hereafter.

There was milk waiting outside the back door every morning, delivered by a milkman who made his rounds by cover of night. The milk was pasteurized, but not homogenized, and the cream naturally rose to the top of the bottles. During the winter, the milk bottles left outside on the steps would have a chance to freeze and the cardboard caps would pop off, pushed up by a tower of frozen cream. The trick was to break off the frozen cream that was sticking out of the top of the bottle and eat it. If you replaced the cap no one would suspect. The end result, however, would be skim milk. On mornings when oatmeal was served and cream was required, adjustments had to be made to my routine.

Coffee at that time was only a commodity and not the gourmet drink of today. It mattered not which brand you bought because it all tasted the same. It was as if all the coffee beans imported into the country were mixed in a giant vat and then sold in various cans labeled "A&P," "Maxwell House" or "Chock full o'Nuts."

To make his coffee, Uncle Oscar had an old, enameled-blue as I remember, percolator. The inside parts were missing so the coffee boiled rather than perked. There was something about adding eggshells to the brew to settle the grounds, but I don't believe it ever worked. It was an acquired knack to sip the coffee and strain the coffee grounds through your teeth, but the taste was worth it.

Even after reaching man's estate, I would sometimes stop into the old place on my way to work, grab a slice of crispy bacon and get outside a cup of Uncle Oscar's coffee. Though separated by two generations, our memories had brushed some common years and the halcyon atmosphere in that kitchen was still the same, always welcoming and safe.

What I wouldn't give today for a cup of that coffee and one of my grandmother's homemade doughnuts.

Hot Pants

It was the winter of my fifth year at the Blue Hill Consolidated School. My desk was near the back, next to the steam radiator. The radiators in the classroom were of the cast iron variety, measuring at least eight feet long and weighing about the same as a small dump truck. The steam was provided by a coal boiler in the basement and, depending on the mood of the janitor whose job it was to stoke the fire, the radiators were either boiling hot or ice cold.

The temperature in the classroom was regulated, not by a thermostat, but by opening and closing various windows. This was a task that could legally be done by the teacher, armed with a longish pole with a hook on one end which, when inserted correctly into the top sash and a bit of physics applied, accomplished the necessary. Due to atmospheric conditions and various ghosts that haunted the place, often only one window in the lot could be manipulated in the manner mentioned, the others being stuck shut. The one window to which I refer was the front one, next to the teacher's desk.

Never known for exhibiting much in the way of sartorial aptitude, my winter school attire consisted of a pair of heavy green wool pants, rubber packs and a plaid flannel shirt. On this particular morning the pants and boots were soaked from a morning snowball fight and while sitting in math class, listening to the proper way of doing the train problem (you know the one), I became aware of steam rising from certain parts of my person. The janitor was apparently on the job and the radiator was performing as advertised.

The wool pants, a few moments earlier having been frozen as stiff as a board, were now reacting to the influence of the radiator. That the pants were beginning to dry out I first considered to be a good thing. It wasn't until we were almost to that part of the lesson where train "A" traveling east from Chicago at 50 mph was about to collide with train "B" traveling west, that matters in the pants department started to become unbearable.

As the blackboard equation progressed, the trains got closer, and the steam kept billowing from those wool pants. Things were heating up. Just as "x" was about to be solved and the teacher was asking for volunteers to provide the missing ingredient, the heat became unbearable. At that time students did not enjoy the "free range" classroom atmosphere that seems so prevalent in this enlightened age. Then, it was unacceptable—a terrible wrath to befall anyone who left their seat without permission.

Much as Dante, as he was led through the various layers of the Underworld by the poet Virgil, must have felt upon reaching the seventh circle, I, too, was feeling consumed by the heat. Arising like a phoenix from the ashes and behaving much like an excited tango dancer, I expect that the teacher's first impression was that I had solved the matter of the trains and was anxious to share this information with the class. Class participation was entirely out of character for me and it took her but an instant to realize that her first impression was in error.

My previous four-year tenure at school did little to support anything I could offer in the way of a defense for my actions and the necessity for some quick thinking on my part seemed in order. The only course of action, given the urgency of the situation, was to use the "may I be excused to visit the men's room" plea. By this time the general decorum of the class was starting to deteriorate, the giggles of the fairer gender and the open guffaws of the boys threatening to turn the proceedings into a state of bedlam in very short order.

The teacher gave her permission almost immediately and I legged it into the hall and continued on to the "basement" where I was able, in some privacy, to remove the lower upholstery and allow the remaining steam to ventilate naturally into the stagnant air of the boys locker room. In due season, I made my way back to the classroom and resumed my seat— walking the while, eyes down-turned, so as to avoid the stares of my classmates and the penetrating gaze of the teacher, who by now had had time to think things over, but still hadn't quite figured it all out.

The saving grace was, for once, the clock, which indicated that recess was just minutes away. Freedom waited without. It was cold that day and it really felt good after the radiator incident. In the space of a quarter hour the green pants had taken on the aspect of two stovepipes about my legs, frozen solid, unbendable at the knee.

Thirty minutes passed quickly, the bell rang and I walked stiff-legged into the hall. The teacher was among those present and it was plain that she desired an explanation for my previous actions. I found myself deposited in the "office" and offered a vacant chair. Reaching down and tapping about the knees confirmed my fears. This would be a time for thinking on my feet. The green pants were still frozen, and though the spirit was willing, sitting would have to wait for them to thaw. The details of the interview remain foggy, but I did spend the afternoon working on the train problem and, just in case you are ever asked…

The trains come together at exactly 12 p.m.

The Ice Nave

Old Man Winter had pulled up his slacks and gotten down to business in no uncertain matter. The snow came on school vacation, just in time to be appreciated by all right-minded boys, particularly those lucky enough to live in Blue Hill.

The day after Christmas found my friend David hard at work assembling a scale model of Sputnik in accordance to the plans that came with his new Erector Set. A remarkable likeness, of course, but he soon realized, as the snow melted from my rubber packs, that just outside there was adventure to be had.

Santa had been generous to me that year. The official Boy Scout hatchet was strapped to the regulation woven belt with brass clamp buckle. On my left hip a new canteen, with a genuine canvas cover, and a four-cell flashlight balanced the heft of the hatchet. In case of an emergency, a Kamp King Jackknife, the deluxe version with spoon and fork, and optional awl, was secreted in my pants pocket.

We headed deep into the woods behind the grammar school, stopping near the Mill Brook. It was the perfect spot for a camp, a brush camp.

The new hatchet hewed poles for the frame. Boughs of fir covered the outside and lined the floor on the inside. When finished, the structure resembled a green igloo. Entering through a low opening that served as a door found us admiring our work and commenting that this was the best one yet.

Gray clouds shrouded the mountain as we broke camp and headed home. The air smelled like snow and snow promised adventure.

The next morning the drift outside my bedroom windowsill was over three feet deep.

There was hot rolled-oats cereal with cream and brown sugar for breakfast. Two full bowls just met the situation. On a cold morning there is nothing like the warm inner glow provided by hot rolled oats and cream.

Dressing for the weather, the outer upholstery comprised heavy green woolen pants, rubber packs, a parka, an Elmer

Fudd hat with earflaps and my grandmother's hand knit mittens. Freedom awaited without. This winter's day was about to be seized.

It was a lonely walk through the streets of the village. No cars were about. With the mercury near zero and the wind a gale out of the north, the snow blew back in the road faster than the town crew could plow it out. It was the kind of day where you knew not even the bright sunshine could warm up the Montréal Express.

The woods seemed different after the storm. An unworldly landscape of snow-covered trees towered about us. Our conversation quieted to a whisper. It was as though we had entered the vestibule of an unfamiliar church.

David spotted our camp, barely a bump of white in the landscape. Digging through the drift with our hands we found the door opening. The inside was dark at first until our eyes adjusted to the silver-green light filtering through the roof. Imperceptibly, the interior grew warmer. The north winds lashed the outside, but the thick layer of snow covering the evergreen boughs kept them at bay.

(This boyhood experience provided me with the knowledge that, when surveying way back in the Maine forests, given my ax and a stand of fir trees, it would be possible to survive a stormy winter's night, perhaps with a certain amount of comfort, hunkered down in a brush camp.)

Camp rations were pure boy food. A peanut butter and marshmallow fluff sandwich, four of my grandmother's homemade doughnuts, a bag of Humpty Dumpty potato chips, two bottles of Coca-Cola (which froze immediately upon being opened) and two Heath candy bars for dessert.

It was soon warm enough to remove our coats. Lying back, we talked of things that mattered. Moot questions, but well worth the asking in 1958.

What if we were the last two people left on earth?

What was the big deal about girls, anyway?

What was it like to be old?

The food and relaxing conversation had their effect. Time slowed to a crawl. Waking from a momentary nap, the fluorescent dial of my Timex showed the lateness of the hour.

Winter's dark comes early in Maine. The four-cell flashlight guided us along the old fishing path beside the Mill Brook, past the silence of a summer swimming hole, Dianna's Pool, and finally to the cut between the two fields behind the school.

We were late and the foreshadow of impending doom when we got home pushed us both to a dead run down Mill Street until we parted company at the corner by the department store.

Supper was on the table as an out-of-breath boy pushed through the kitchen door.

My grandmother's look was one of worry, anger and relief, all rolled into one. Uncle Oscar just smiled.

Saps

Snow still stood deep but the corpuscles were coursing rapidly through my young veins, fizzing like a mouthful of hot Pepsi. It was Sunday morning and making my way down a path cut through a forlorn snowdrift, the residue of a February nor'easter, found me in Uncle Oscar's shop.

The woodstove was hard at work, and so was Uncle Oscar. "Sap's runnin'," he said, not looking up from the bench on which were laid out an assortment of odd-looking wooden sticks. "Spouts," he replied in answer to my unvoiced question. Now at least they had a name, but what the heck were they? There were also a dozen or so large, empty coffee cans with wire bails attached.

One lesson learned from Uncle Oscar was to wait and watch. In time, all would be revealed.

A half-inch bit and a bitbrace were taken from their place above the bench. The cans and spouts were collected and we were off to the great outdoors. The night before had been cold, but this morning the spring sun had already sent the mercury well above the freezing mark.

We came to an ancient tree. Uncle Oscar fitted the bit into the bitbrace and leaned it into the trunk. The handle cranked. The razor-sharp bit cut cleanly through the gnarly bark and continued on into pure white sapwood. A moment later the white wood chips were joined by a freshet of cold maple sap, the raw, sweet essence of spring eternal. As the river Pison flowed out of Eden, bringing gold to the land of Havilah, so would this elixir bring, in due season, gold to the leaves of this noble Ent.

Uncle Oscar backed out the bit, the cold sap wetting the fingertips of his left hand. Raising his fingers to his lips brought a smile to his weathered face. "Puts me in mind of when I was a boy."

As the observer, the lesson went something like this. Find a spot on the sunny side of a maple tree; one below a large branch is best. Using the bitbrace, bore a hole into the trunk about two inches deep. Catch some cold maple sap in your fingers and taste it. Smile. Drive a wooden spout into the hole; the groove in the top provides a sap channel and a notch holds the wire bail. Listen to the steady drip-drip-drip echo on the bottom of the collection can.

After a few more instructional trees, I was loosed to find and tap enough more to deplete the remaining inventory of cans and spouts. The first trick in tapping trees is to make sure you are tapping a maple tree. Not as easy as it sounds. With no leaves, only the bark and the shape of the tree to make the determination, I bored into more than one oak or ash before the chips finally came out wet and sweet.

Every afternoon after school I collected the day's bounty in two ten-quart pails and delivered them to my grandmother's kitchen. The steaming canners worked night and day on top of the range. Exactly how much sap is required per stack of pancakes is a question that science must have answered years ago. My observation was "a lot more than you'd think."

The great thing about the process of boiling down sap, besides the obvious syrup that resulted, was the aroma of that sweet steam. No part of the house escaped. It was like living in a candy factory. The new "As seen on TV" Ronco Humidifier had nothing on a canner of simmering maple sap to give a boost to the ambient humidity of a house.

One morning the sunshine waxed scarlet on the tips of the maple whips and the meager harvest had acquired a bitter cast. Too soon, sap season was finished. By tomorrow morning the sap in the canners would have rendered sufficiently to be put up in mason jars and added, with the others, to the pantry shelf at the top of the cellar stairs.

By evening, the effervescence in the young master's blood had quieted to a degree. Sleep was quick to come—a sleep of the kind reserved to youth, filled with sweet, maple-flavored dreams.

I awoke with the sun. The smell of coffee and bacon frying, mingled with that sweet aroma of Spring, met me as I came down the stairs. It was as my foot struck the last, or possibly, the next to the last, stair tread, that I became aware that something was amiss. In the years since I've recognized that this sensation warrants attention.

Uncle Oscar was standing by the stove, a cup of black Maxwell House in hand, staring intently at—the wall. Feeling flatter than an open bottle of Pepsi on the day after the picnic, my eyes followed his gaze and the object of his attention soon became obvious.

The previous winter my grandmother had papered the kitchen, a lively pattern, you'd recognize it, the one consisting of vines and brightly colored flowers. She had hung it herself using a paste of her own invention made from flour, salt and some secret ingredients.

When you think of wallpaper you naturally picture it as actually attached to the wall. At present, this was not entirely the case. Although some was still connected, the majority was either hanging or had fallen off completely and was lying conspicuously on the cupboards and floor.

"It was the steam from the sap. Your grandmother is sure going to be mad." Uncle Oscar had a way of stating the obvious.

The suggestion was made that the mousetraps we had set last fall at camp needed to be checked. A second glance about the room confirmed the wisdom of this strategy. Uncle Oscar's Model A awaited without.

Eventually, repairs to the kitchen were made. I helped. All agreed that the new pattern was far superior to the previous one; springish, I believe was the adjective used.

I don't remember another spring spent in a similar manner. Like a ne'er-do-well relative, the subject of tapping trees was never mentioned in family conversations.

Guardian Angel

It seems, of late, that Guardian Angels have fallen from favor. There are some who will argue that there is no such thing as a Guardian Angel and if the truth be known, these people probably don't have one. Guardian Angels, like the rest of us, appreciate a little recognition once in a while and without it they no doubt become discouraged.

At a very young age, a Guardian Angel was most certainly assigned to me. The fact that you are reading these words is proof enough, even for the staunchest disbeliever, to stand corrected.

First, a little history. In my youth, Blue Hill Bay froze solid from about John's Island in. By late winter it was a common sight to see smelt tents, looking for all the world like little houses on a Monopoly board, scattered about bay ice.

A smelt tent was very similar to the ice shack one sees on local ponds, except they were infinitely more practical in their construction. A smelt tent was built on a light wooden frame. This frame was covered with cloth, probably canvas from an old sail, or perhaps a bed sheet, and painted gray. I don't believe a smelt tent had a floor but the paint formed a barrier against the wind. Inside there was a little tin stove. Such stoves were available at any hardware store and ranged in size from a 10-quart pail to a half barrel. The latter was used to heat many a hunting camp while the former was just perfect for a smelt tent. A length of stovepipe extended through the roof and an armload of kindling brought the smelt tent up to temperature in less than five minutes. A hole was cut in the ice and the smelts were fished. It was not uncommon for a frying pan and a dollop of lard to complete the process. Though never consumed in my presence, it was often customary to wash the smelts down with a modicum of alcoholic stimulants.

Whether or not these were the same smelts that ran in the brooks later that spring I cannot say, but I expect they were. One never knows the mind of a smelt. Perhaps they were biding their time under the bay ice until open water in the streams.

As spring progressed, walking on the ice was not recommended. The rising and falling of the tide cracked the floe and created ice cakes. These were floating slabs of ice approximately a foot thick. It was a sport for David and me, on a high tide, to "jump ice cakes" from the town wharf across the cove to ring rock. I had been told repeatedly not to do such a thing, but...

The high tide that Saturday afternoon found David and self playing hopscotch on the brine.

We were almost all the way across when the corner of an ice cake gave way beneath the weight of my boot. It is amazing how cold water can be when it is thrust about your person on a March afternoon, particularly when the cold water in question has had the better part of a Maine winter to become that way.

Feeling severely hampered by my inability to swim and my weighty sartorial attire I went down.

Down, down, down into the depths of which nightmares are made and all hope is lost.

This was an instance where my Guardian Angel came into play. In the trough of a wave my toes touched bottom just inches before my nose touched the water. Frantically pushing ice cakes to and fro and running like mad I managed to make landfall and drag myself, exhausted, to bare ground.

The afternoon was coming off cold. One fear replaced another. Punishment awaited at home when it became clear what had happened.

It was nearly dark before the courage to return to the house supplanted the sleepy coldness in my body.

Whoever said that if one were to do something one should do it all the way, was right. The good thing about falling in the bay and becoming completely drenched is that one looks about the same from north to south. My wetness was not obvious and nobody even noticed.

In my room the wet packs were suctioned to my feet and my longjohns were frozen as stiff as a board. These soon gave way to a Saturday bath, dry clothes and bedroom slippers.

Sitting beside me in an empty chair, my Guardian Angel joined us that night for supper. Baked beans and yeast rolls never tasted as good.

March Hill

The old timers used to say that there is only one way to get out of a Maine winter and that was to climb "March Hill." I have not heard the phrase in years, but this year it seems most appropriate.

The thing about Maine winters is that they seem to go on forever. They have been known to use up the whole of spring and a good part of what should rightfully be allocated to fall. March has a way of putting a strain on even the most ardent Mainer, not to mention his woodpile. What seemed in the fall to be enough wood to last for ten winters was dwindling away to a degree that, by the Ides, it was burned sparingly lest it be used up too soon. It was often a race which would disappear first, the snow banks at the edge of the fields or the wood pile in the shed.

My friend David had something to show me. His grandparents lived up on the Acre, in a medium-sized yellow house on the edge of the millstream. At the time, the remnants of an old mill dam provided a very substantial pond fronting the house, providing fishing in the summer and skating in the winter.

All these are gone, the dam, the pond, even the house. The brook, however, still threads its way, now unfettered, to the bay.

On the south side of the house there were neatly stacked rows of split firewood, and it was through these that David led me one Saturday morning. My interest was piqued. David was not one to underestimate, but there were exceptions.

Looking around found me at a complete loss. Stove length firewood, a sawhorse, an old chopping block, and a bucksaw were the only things visible to the untrained eye. It was the latter that had created all the excitement. David lifted the saw into the morning sunlight so that it would be better seen. The wooden handles were worn but the teeth on the blade sparkled like a whetted rapier.

A gift from his grandfather, the saw was undoubtedly older than the two of us combined but nonetheless functional. A demonstration was in order. A four-foot length of five-inch maple was placed in the sawhorse. David drew the old saw back and forth against the wood. With ease the bucksaw melted its way through and the end fell to earth. "Ten swipes; sometimes I can do it in seven. You try."

My efforts were not as rewarding. Ten swipes found me panting, and it was a number more before the stick hit the ground.

We took turns, David with the patience of Job explaining the proper technique—and self, working up a sweat. It was not my idea of a grand way to spend Saturday morning.

At the end of an hour's time we had manufactured quite a pile of firewood. Twelve swipes was my best effort. David was still aiming for the elusive seven.

We were about to take a break when David's grandfather, Hollis, was suddenly in our midst. He set a six-inch piece of oak in the horse. We counted—one, two, three, four and a half swipes and the free end landed in the sawdust.

David and I looked at each other in amazement. "How?"

His words were slow and measured, like the rhythm of the bucksaw. "Always remember...let the tool do the work."

Gone Fishing

Like an army defeated;
The snow hath retreated...
The ploughboy is whooping–anon–anon...
There's joy in the mountains;
There's life in the fountains...
The rain is over and gone.

Not one of mine; in fact it was written about 200 years ago by an English poet named William Wordsworth.

The feeling holds as true today as it did then. Spring has that certain something about it—a sense of energy and optimism that has spent the better part of winter napping beside the fireplace. Now that "The snow hath retreated" and there is "life in the fountains," there is only one thing for a Maine boy to do.

Go fishing!

Blue Hill had its share of good trout brooks, "fountains" as Wordsworth called them, and one of the nicest was about five minutes' walk from my kitchen door.

There were three conditions that accompanied the first trout hunt.

First, always obey the law, and the law said open water fishing could begin no earlier than April first.

Second, the ice must be out of the brooks by that date. Often the opening day would find more ice than water in the streams, and it is difficult to find an interested trout in water just this side of frozen.

Third, one needed bait, and bait meant angleworms. As everyone is aware, angleworms live in the ground. And say what you like about the intelligence of angleworms, they do have the good sense to stay down deep enough in the ground to keep from freezing their butts off, if worms actually have butts.

This is where David came in. Somehow, he could find enough worms to supply both of us. It didn't matter if there was two feet of snow on the ground, David would show up with a can of angleworms. Asking him where he found them was always met with a sort of incoherent mumble, followed by a long story about his new Kamp King jackknife.

The neat thing about fishing is that it didn't require too much in the way of financial outlay. Babson and Duffy's was a hardware store in town that carried all the necessary items. One spring we both bought new rods and reels of dubious quality. One of our earliest lessons was never to buy a self-contained reel. You know the kind, where the line winds back into the dark recesses of the reel. Except, there was a two-wind limit, probably engineered into the thing at the factory. On the third wind, especially if there is a fish on the end, the line proceeds to tangle itself, both on the inside and on the outside of the reel. The resulting mess was put on earth to try a boy's soul.

After losing the biggest fish in the whole brook and taking the reel completely apart, the reality dawned that there was no way of ever getting it back together again. The only recourse was to pitch the thing as far as possible into the bushes.

David actually managed to put his reel back together once. But, on the third winding, it popped open like a horse chestnut in a leaf fire.

After that we would tie our lines to a freshly cut maple switch. The arrangement worked almost as well, without the aggravations of technology.

It is interesting that there are some people who are true fishermen. David's uncle, Doug Stover, worked as custodian at the grammar school, as meticulous a man as you would ever care to meet—and could he catch fish! Doug could catch fish where there weren't any fish.

I ran into Doug at the post office a while back and asked him if he did much fishing.

Not as much as he'd like.

I suspect that this April when Spring puts "life in the fountains" you'll see Doug on the bank of the Mill Brook with a fishing rod in one hand and a string of "keepers" in the other.

The Bear Facts

Bear had his own schedule and followed it assiduously each day, at least during the summer months when we boys were at liberty—liberty meaning free from the eight prison cells of the Consolidated School.

Liberty came at length during early June when the yellow buttercups and dandelions sparkled against the green grass of spring. Spring in Blue Hill only takes a couple of days, a week at most, and then summer steps out of the screen door and gets down to business.

Getting back to Bear. Bear, whose given name was Harold, please correct me if this is not the case, was an Osgood. The Osgoods were an old family in Blue Hill and each generation of the Osgood family had a "Cub" and a "Bear." Cub Osgood was a town selectman for many years.

Bear lived in the old Osgood house on Pleasant Street, just above the Baptist Church. Each day at 2:30 in the afternoon he walked down to the village and purchased two bottles of beer from Merrill and Hinckley's store. With his prize secreted in a brown paper bag, he walked down the hill to the firehouse.

The firehouse then was in approximately the same location as it is now. It was a wooden structure with a sort of tower on top. This tower housed a siren, which everyone called the "fire whistle." When a fire was called in, someone would blow the fire whistle and the men around town would put aside their labors and man the fire trucks. This is still the case today, but the fire whistle is no more.

The old firehouse was never locked and it was through the side door that one Bear and two beers passed each weekday afternoon. We boys were under the impression that Mrs. Bear did not condone the consumption of alcoholic stimulants in her home and that was the reason for Bear's daily visits.

Bear had led a fantastic life. He was an engineer and came out of retirement in the mid-1960s to work on the highway design when South Street was rebuilt from a single lane dirt road to its present state.

He had traveled the world, but his main claim to fame was baseball. Bear played professional baseball in his youth, perhaps for the Cleveland Indians. In fact, his generation had produced a number of professional baseball players from the Blue Hill area.

Bear was full of stories that he would relate to anyone who would listen. Stories of defending a hilltop in Cuba by throwing stones at the enemy when his ammunition ran out, or perhaps the time he struck out Babe Ruth. Bear had a noticeable stammer when he told these stories and often a single afternoon was not long enough for him to complete the unedited versions.

At 4 o'clock Bear would always head home. He would leave the firehouse not at 3:59, nor at 4:01. He would always leave at exactly 4 o'clock. It was a game with us to divert his attention so that he would miss the 4 o'clock deadline, but we never succeeded.

For years we heard these fantastic accounts over and over again until that one summer when both Bear and our boyhood were gone.

It is with regret that those stories were heard through a boy's ears and quickly forgotten. To hear them again? In a dream, perhaps.

Fishin' and Fly Dope

"When the alder leaf is the size of a mouse's ear, the blackflies will soon appear." Not one of my sayings.

It is odd sometimes how a certain smell can bring back an old, forgotten memory. The next time you are in the neighborhood of a box of crayons, take a whiff; you'll see.

The particular aroma that recently excited the old gray matter to snap to attention was that of citronella. As bug season approached, Uncle Oscar's neckwear always included a bandana soaked in the stuff. In the days before DEET, people made their own concoctions to repel blackflies and mosquitoes, the idea being that the worse it smelled, the better it worked.

Some of the preparations contained ingredients such as kerosene, tar oil, camphor, sulfur, garlic and whiskey. Some thought that the latter, for the best results, should be applied straight, both liberally and internally. I am reminded of a story of a prominent landscape artist, of the Monhegan school, who, while having a show at the Ladies Social Library in Blue Hill, was asked by one of the social ladies, given the uniqueness of his work, if there were any special art supplies that he relied on in creating his masterpieces. "Yes, indeed," he replied, "most times it's a toss-up between whiskey and fly dope."

There was a commercial insect repellent product available at the time called 6-12. It resembled a large tube of ChapStick. It had a great marketing approach. It went on greasy and had a fragrance that would actually attract the flies, with the result that you needed to apply even more. It also was likely, if left for a time on the dashboard, to melt into a pool of foul-smelling grease. If the car windows were cracked, the pool of grease would soon be infused with flies that had become stuck in the goop. To my certain knowledge 6-12 is no longer available wherever the better class of fly dope is sold.

The homemade potions had varying degrees of effectiveness. Most worked entirely on the psychological level. The fact that they didn't work at all in repelling bugs was of no particular relevance to the user, as the human mind has a wonderful capacity for denial and black flies require as much denial as one's mind can manufacture. This "bug dope" or "fly dope," as it was known, was immune to soap and water, with a lasting fragrance that often lingered on one's person well into deer season. When freshly applied, it had the added benefit of keeping most other humans at a comfortable distance.

I say "benefit," but there are exceptions. Uncle Oscar related a story from the days of his youth, pre-Model A, when transportation was by horse and buggy. The Grange social was well attended and the trip home after the event looked promising. The young lady was attractive, the night mild and the moon full. Her father, however, was a methodical man, the sort of man who kept clocks. Uncle Oscar had observed a rather prominent specimen of the grandfather variety standing picket in the front hall.

Aware to the minute of how long it took to travel the distance from the Grange Hall to the farm, the father would abide no funny business. This time restraint precluded the young couple from pausing along the way to do any sightseeing. But, a good horse, as I understand, can find its own way home with little or no human input, leaving the driver with time to pursue whatever cultural endeavor seemed appropriate. The conversation had just turned to Keats when the young lady in question suddenly developed an inappropriate allergy to citronella. The syncopation of the steady clip-clop of the horse's hooves coupled with the staccato sneezes of the delicately nurtured, cut the night air like a rapier, twisting the while in the young man's heart. No business resulted.

The Model A slowed and came to a halt under an apple tree next to Bragdon's Brook. With the windows down, a Model A can easily outrun the smell of citronella but with the air suddenly still, the olfactories were once again overpowered. Dust from the dirt road swirled about while the resident black flies gathered for the feast. A reminder from Uncle Oscar as I swatted a particularly aggressive specimen who had attached itself to my left ear: "Now a hundred more will come to the funeral."

A worm was fitted to a hook and the pole placed in my hands. The line drifted to a patch of froth where an eddy circled around a rock. There was a tug on the line that nearly yanked the pole from my hands. " Easy, easy...reel him in easy." After a dozen or so more "easys," I had a beauty.

Some men might remember their first kiss but I suspect all men remember their first trout.

David and I were best friends and when trout season opened on April 1, we were among the first to the task. Often on opening day, ice was still in the brooks, and patches of snow lingered, couched in spots of shade. In spite of this, David could always find worms for bait. Though David and I did our best, trout fishing is an ancient art that is not given; it must be won. It would always amaze me that David and I could fish a certain brook, extracting one or two "brookies" that were barely keepers, and David's uncle Doug would follow along behind us and come home with his limit. Doug Stover is one of the best brook fishermen I have ever known.

The Blue Hill area has some great trout brooks—break out the citronella, dig a few worms and give it a whirl. Like homemade fly dope, fishing works mainly on the psychological level. An idle hour well spent.

Time is but the stream I go a-fishing in. I drink at it; but while I drink, I see the sandy bottom and detect how shallow it is. Its thin current slides away, but eternity remains...
—Henry David Thoreau

Beauty

There comes a time in the life of a boy that his thoughts turn to higher and nobler things. How had I not noticed her before? Her beauty was beyond the art of even the bards of old to describe. Mere words could never do justice to such as she. Even a song couldn't come close. My being worthy of such a beautiful thing was a question that crossed my mind. Upon quick reflection, the answer was obvious. My not being worthy? What a foolish notion!

With time, I could think of nothing else. My schoolwork, not that it was ever my top priority, began to suffer as my every waking thought revolved around her. Even food seemed to lose its former fascination.

I had her picture. It was secreted, where it would never be discovered, between pages 56 and 57 of the Hardy Boys mystery What Happened at Midnight—you remember the one where Joe Hardy disappears at midnight and there were jewel thieves, and...but I digress.

At night, I would bring her picture out of hiding and pull the covers over my head. My official Boy Scout flashlight provided the necessary illumination. Closing my eyes now, the picture is as clear as it was those many years ago, seared forever in my memory.

She had chrome fenders, a bright red frame, whitewall tires, sweptback handlebars with the colored plastic strips that flowed in the breeze, and a genuine leatherette saddle. These features all gave her a certain class that lifted her high above the norm, but it was the electric-powered headlight that really caught my eye. It ran by a small generator attached to the front wheel. The faster one peddled, the brighter the light! How cool was that?

One of life's lessons is, that, often, beautiful things come with a price, and this particular price was $24.99 plus freight. Every cent was saved toward this end. Lawns were mowed, snow was shoveled, wood was stacked and any chore, no matter how disagreeable, was done in an effort to amass the necessary funds.

I was less than a dollar short, with no prospects, when Uncle Oscar came to the rescue. It was in the form of a two-week advance on my lawn-mowing contract. The order blank from the Montgomery Ward catalog had been filled out for months and it was the work of a moment for me to run across the street to the post office. Ward Snow was postmaster and he helped count the money and filled out the paperwork for the money order.

Now, all I had to do was wait. And, wait I did! It seemed like years, but in late July word came down from Dodge's Express that the shipment had arrived. It was a Saturday afternoon and Howard Dodge had made his final trip from Bangor with the bicycle on board. One of the tires was a little slack but Howard's garage contained many hand-operated tire pumps. By the process of elimination we found one that still worked and within minutes the whitewalls bulged smartly under the chrome fenders.

The evening was a little on the cool side as I snapped the kickstand back and spun the rear tire on the dirt of the driveway. Supper would have to keep. This was the maiden

voyage, the shakedown cruise. Let's see what this baby was made of!

A hill was what was needed and fortunately Blue Hill village is surrounded by them. Tenney seemed to call us. At the time Tenney Hill was a two-lane affair with deep ruts that passed for ditches on either side. We reached the top by the back way, up Union Street and across Beech Hill Road. Traffic was non-existent as we sat at the top. Excitement bubbled in me like an Alka-Seltzer commercial. We were higher than the steeple on the Congo Church. At that moment the bike came to life. If ever a machine had a soul, she did.

As Uncle Oscar always said, "God hates a coward," and neither the bike nor I would claim ownership to cowardice. A couple of strong cranks on the pedals set her in motion and after a second or two there was no keeping up, so we coasted. Tenney Hill dipped a little, then flattened out for a stretch. Another dip and we were breaking the speed limit. It crossed my mind that a handlebar-mounted speedometer should be the first accessory. My baseball cap flew off my head and was gone forever. Our speed was increasing with each passing second. Goggles would be my second accessory. It's a nuisance when your ears get filled with water from your eyes.

The church flew by on my right and the time had come to rein this filly in. Up to this point, brakes had been of little consequence because the first part of the voyage had been all uphill. Now brakes were what were needed to bring this adventure to a happy conclusion. This particular model bicycle had come equipped with coaster brakes, the kind where you push the pedal backwards and the rear wheel stops the machine. Applying the necessary backward pressure produced no results. The brakes were not operating as advertised. Even worse, they were not operating at all.

"Now, Beauty! [This was her name.] This is no time to kid around!" Some bicycles love to go fast and it was obvious that Beauty fell into this category. This was her first outing and she was enjoying her newfound freedom. Starting to panic, I jumped up and down on the brake pedal, but nothing happened. We were not slowing down, but going even faster.

Through wind-watered eyes Main Street loomed like a tunnel of doom. Hollis Stover pulled his '49 Plymouth out of Mill Street. Beauty and I streaked toward them like a torpedo toward the side of a battleship. I jumped down on the brake pedal with all my weight. "Beauty!!! Stop!!!" I screamed at the top of my voice. There was a cracking sound from the rear brake hub and the back tire suddenly locked up. Smoke was boiling from the rubber tire, but we were finally slowing down. Leaning Beauty hard over to the left we grazed the massive silver fenders of the Plymouth, stopping just past the gas pumps at the Esso station.

It took a good thirty seconds or so for my heart to stop pounding. What a ride!

Uncle Oscar was there as I parked Beauty in the barn.

"How'd you like your new bike?"

"Just swell!"

Decoration Day

Uncle Oscar called it "Decoration Day" and for as long as anyone can remember, on the last day of May, Blue Hill held its Memorial Day Parade. Sometime in the early 1970s, Congress passed the National Holiday Act to shift traditional holidays to a convenient Monday, but this story happened before that.

If you have seen one Memorial Day parade, you have a fairly good idea what they are. Very little has changed over the years.

On the morning of the parade the whole extended family, including friends and neighbors, would congregate on the large piazza that wrapped around two sides of the old house. Some would sit in the porch chairs, some on the stone steps, but most would stand as tall as they could. It was a day for standing tall.

As a young boy, the report of the rifle salute at the Mill Brook bridge would send me running to the safety of the kitchen with my hands over my ears. As years passed, my outward poltroonery abated, but even today, a close observer might detect my sudden start at the command, "FIRE!"

The air on Main Street was charged like a thunderstorm on an August afternoon. The high school band led off the festivities. If George Stevens Academy wasn't up to the task then Bucksport might be called in.

The honor guard of veterans would follow in step. In my earlier memories, representatives of the Great War, WWI, would be marching beside their comrades from WWII.

World War II was still fresh in people's memory. Sadness and understanding respect mingled with relief and pride. When the color guard passed, a hush came over the crowd, hats were removed, and hands were placed on hearts.

Following in open automobiles were dignitaries, local and imported, all with the practiced wave and smile that is part and parcel of the nib profession.

The Boy Scouts put in an appearance just ahead of the fire trucks. Allen Mello was also a yearly fixture. In his ubiquitous way, he somehow managed to be everywhere at once.

Bringing up the rear were the youngsters on bicycles. This was my favorite part. To ride a bicycle in the parade was my dream. I had previously been hampered by the official entry

criteria requiring a bicycle. One must first possess a bicycle, and the bicycle must be decorated. After all, it was Decoration Day.

It was the spring following the summer of my new bicycle. "Beauty" was her name. She was red with chrome fenders, whitewall tires, coaster brakes and a genuine leatherette saddle. Beauty had spent the winter in the barn along with the leaf rakes and fishing rods.

Some of you might think that decorating a bicycle is an easy thing to do. That's because you have never had to do it. Crepe paper is the preferred method. Cut into strips of red, white and blue and carefully woven between the spokes and wrapped around the handlebars, the effect was absolutely astounding.

May 30 dawned bright and sunny. The lark was still rubbing his eyes and yawning as I pushed Beauty into the driveway. My new white sneakers, Red Ball Keds, complemented by matching white socks, lit up the whole dooryard. Walking on sunshine.

Tenney Hill was blocked off while Beauty and self, along with twenty or thirty other kids, waited for the big event. It wasn't until after the ceremony at the bridge that the bicycle brigade was allowed to proceed.

It was soon brought to my attention that we were expected to ride slowly. Beauty was built for speed and slow was not in her vocabulary. The other factor that soon dawned was that the parade seemed to stop at intervals for no apparent reason. Beauty was a full-sized bike and the idea was that I would grow into it. The fact remained that when straddling the crossbar my short legs couldn't reach the ground. This was an awkward and potentially painful embarrassing situation. Only youth could have adapted to the gymnast's practiced dismount, which I found necessary when the parade stopped abruptly.

All was proceeding well. The report of the volleys echoed from the mountain. The band struck a lively patriotic note and things were moving forward in a regular, if not speedy, fashion. There seemed to be an urgency to cover the quarter mile to the cemetery like Babe Snow's pacer at the last sulky race on Labor Day.

The piazza was full of people and it seemed all eyes were on me. A nib wave was in order. My right hand loosed its grip from the tasseled handle bar and shot skyward. At this very instant the parade came to an abrupt stop.

If you have ever played dominoes, not the real game, but the fun part where you stand them on end and tip the first one over and it knocks down another and another and another, then you have a good idea of the resulting chain of events.

Beauty ran into David's bike. David in turn knocked over Joe's, and within less than a minute there wasn't a bicycle standing.

71

For a moment, confusion reigned. That I was the cause of this catastrophe was lost for the moment on the participants. No one was hurt, save for my skinned elbow and Beauty's bent fender. David started to laugh. Glances were exchanged, and he was soon joined by the rest of us.

By the time the bicycles had been righted, the body of the parade was disappearing into the distance. We may have been down, but we were not out. After all, we were from Blue Hill.

As one well-oiled machine, with David in the lead and Beauty a close second, the bicycles closed the distance to the parade in record time. The Tour de France could have taken our correspondence course.

Uncle Oscar always said that all experience is a lesson. To paraphrase, "There is a time to wave, and a time to keep your hands on the handlebars."

Carnations and Rosebuds

Uncle Oscar called them "grand" days. A minimum of three and a maximum of 11 are allotted to the state of Maine annually. They nearly always fall in September, usually around the time of the Blue Hill Fair. It was the morning of one of these days that found me zipping along a familiar road in the old Ford pickup. The windows were rolled down and the radio cranked to the oldies station. The Lovin' Spoonful was asking if I believed in magic. It's hard not to believe in magic on a Grand Day.

Pondering the magic question, there came into my view, ahead on the shoulder of the road, a rather substantial animal. Perhaps it was Puff the magic dragon, as was now being suggested by the radio. Time would tell. Reining the Ford in a mite we slowed to a crawl. Puff it was not, unless Puff was actually a heifer. The possibility seemed remote.

In my youth, seeing a heifer standing by the side of the road was not an uncommon occurrence, but it has been years since my last sighting. Ths heifer looked completely at ease, chewing the delicious grass in a decidedly contented manner. Remembering the old advertising slogan, "Carnation, milk from contented cows," the thought crossed my mind that it is difficult to find a cow that isn't contented.

Cows, particularly heifers, are not the most intelligent of animals and, considering the traffic, my concern mounted for Puff's safety. From the driveway across the road there appeared an old farmer, and he was cutting out a good pace in our direction. He couldn't have been better cast if this had been a Hollywood movie. His costume was perfect, complete with whiskers, overalls and a straw hat. Time seemed to stop for an instant and then wind backwards 50 years or so. The windshield of my truck was transformed into the screen of an old Philco television. Gunsmoke was on, and there was Chester, rope in hand, ambling along after Marshall Dillon. A moment later the farmer had a lead on the errant bovine. Gunsmoke faded, and the grand day continued.

Thoughts of Carnation milk and contented cows, when left to ruminate in one's head on a grand day, often evolve in odd ways. From a store of nearly forgotten memories, Rosebud popped to the surface. Rosebud was a heifer that left a vivid impression on my young mind. As heifers go, she was enormous and anything but contented. For an animal of her size, she could sure run.

The Grindles lived about a half mile down the road and they always kept a cow for milk. The mysteries of dairy farming escape me but I suspect that milk cows need replacing occasionally and Rosebud was probably intended as a back-up.

Rosebud spent her days patrolling the pasture. Like the Minotaur from the island of Crete, Rosebud would have liked nothing more that to chase down unsuspecting boys and devour them alive.

It was a grand day and Jack and I were taking a shortcut through the Grindles' lower pasture, our final destination being a favorite pool in the brook. About half way across the field the look on Jack's face told me something was definitely wrong.

Jack did not scare easily, but the reason for his concern soon became apparent. Rosebud was standing at the top of the hill looking intently in our direction.

It is a good policy in circumstances such as this to swap time for distance, and to that end we both took off toward the fence on a dead run. Jack took the early lead, but my adrenalin soon cut in and the distance between us lessened. Rosebud's four feet were more than equal to our two and she was closing fast. With a sudden burst of speed Jack reached the fence and, like Superman, leapt it in a single bound. With Jack shouting encouragement from the safety of the barbwire and Rosebud's hot breath on the back of my neck, I said a prayer to whomever may have been listening at the time and gave it my all.

To those of you familiar with cow pastures it is not necessary to tell you what sort of things one finds scattered about on the ground. Cow flap is the polite name and these flaps come in various stages of freshness. It was just as Rosebud had gained the advantage in the race when my left foot landed in a particularly fresh and slippery flap. Exactly what transpired in the next couple of seconds remains a mystery. There was a feeling of floating and a sudden crash. Somehow, as if by magic, I found myself standing next to Jack on the safe side of the fence. I was a little the worse for wear, the seat of my dungarees was covered with slimy stuff that didn't smell all that great, and the collar of my shirt was torn from the barbwire—a small price to pay for such a great adventure.

With the fence now between us, a disappointed Rosebud turned back up the hill.

The Summer of '64

Often, the beginning of a story starts long before the actual story part. This story began in mid winter of 1964.

The author was serving out his sentence in the back row of the study hall at George Stevens Academy. This study hall was a large room at the top of the stairs in the original GSA building. It had south facing windows that afforded a view of the snowflakes sifting down from a cold gray sky. The American History textbook was the perfect size for one to conceal a far more interesting issue of magazine. In the back pages of this particular issue was a classified section. My attention was arrested by an illustrated advertisement for boat plans. The boats shown were sporty little outboard runabouts. They came in a variety of sizes and according to the ad they "could be constructed from plywood, for fun and or profit, using common hand tools" The cost for a set of plans, or blueprints, to facilitate the building process, was five dollars.

At that point in my career my love life was in the tank. Before class that morning my current girlfriend had handed me the mitten. It was not the first time a similar thing had happened and it was certainly not to be the last. Not to imply that all womankind is fickle, but this was one of life's lessons. The reason given was my lack of an automobile, or for that matter even a driver's license. Her affections were drawn elsewhere, to someone who was aptly supplied with both.

You may be wondering, what does this segue have to do

with the boat? Well, the simple fact was that the five dollars, which had been earmarked to be spent on a double date with the girl in question, could now be put toward the boat plans.

That Saturday morning found me at the post office with Postmaster Ward Snow filling out the form for a money order. The addition of a five-cent stamp completed the transaction. All that was left now was to wait.

Within the month a parcel arrived. There was no doubt that this had been five dollars well spent. Words like "stem," "chine" and "transom" leaped from the pages of the carefully detailed instruction manual. However, studying the weighty tome beneath the covers by flashlight that night quenched my initial enthusiasm like a campfire in a thunderstorm. My previous experience in building was limited to model airplanes that were made of balsa wood and paper with rubber band-powered propellers. Building a real boat was not the same sort of thing at all.

The next evening at supper my boat was a topic of discussion. There is nothing like getting outside a slice of my grandmother's apple pie to raise one's spirits and by the second iteration my spirits were right up there with Chuck Yeager.

Uncle Oscar asked to look at the plans. He studied them carefully for the space of one and a half cigarettes. "Let's go down to the shop," he suggested.

Uncle Oscar's workshop, or "shop" is still there. It is that small shingled building just to the left of Peter Clapp's garage. At the time it was stocked with tools and lumber was stacked in the rafters, just waiting to be made into something useful. A boat came to mind. We built a fire and set to clear a place to work.

I suspect that just about anyone who grew up on the coast of Maine has tried his hand at boatbuilding at least once. The dust of years fell from the boards in the rafters as we sorted through the different sizes and lengths. The boat plans were very particular regarding the type of wood used for the different parts. Uncle Oscar was not so fussy. He assured me that spruce could be substituted for western hemlock and oak would work just fine for the transom knee.

The winter evening wore on and by the time the dust had settled and the wood fire had died back to glowing coals, we had made a good start on the summer of '64.

Have you ever noticed that some of the most seminal events in your life rise out of circumstances over which you have little or no control? Often, at the time, you don't even know what's happening. You begin as a minor character but, as events unfold, by the end of the Agatha Christie mystery you are either the butler who did it or the body found in the library.

The reader will remember that the author, being disadvantaged by age in the way of not having a driver's license, was passed over one midwinter day by his current girlfriend. As any young man will attest, having a girlfriend, even in high school, requires a certain amount of venture capital. The old "heave ho" had the effect of freeing the princely sum of five dollars. This fiver was put toward construction plans for a nifty little outboard motorboat.

The details of construction are lost in time, but the general gist of the thing was that, using the various patterns purchased by mail order, one cut, sawed, glued, screwed and clamped the various wooden pieces of the vessel, one piece to the next, side by each, until in time, an object was created resembling the boat in the final photograph.

All very simple and easy, or so was my belief. The actual construction proved more difficult. Uncle Oscar had allowed me unrestricted use of his shop, including carpentry tools, provided that they were used with respect and put back in their places.

After school and Saturdays would find me in the workshop, rather like Noah building his Ark. The Maine winter was dark and cold but the woodstove, fed by scraps and "mistakes," heated the shop to t-shirt temperature in no time. Bare electric bulbs illuminated the workbench and painted prismatic rainbows on the frost-covered windowpanes.

In the daytime, music from the Bangor stations played through my transistor radio. After dark, Boston stations like WBZ and WMEX would come in. Sometimes late at night, when the wind was out of the north, Murray the K, WINS, New York, would add a certain sophistication to the pedestrian atmosphere of the old shop.

During the initial phase of construction, the plans were of some help but, in hindsight, their accuracy was called into question more that once. Frustration mixed with the sawdust on the shop floor. Boats of my acquaintance had always appeared symmetrical and when the one being built listed to starboard even when perched atop the sawhorses, some adjustments were in order and the detailed plans were destined to a higher calling. Kindling for the wood stove. Without plans to muddy the waters, the project went much smoother.

With only music for company, the winter evenings drifted toward spring and the ice-packed path to the shop gave way to mud. The boat took shape with her lines no longer governed by the working plans but by the eye of her maker. It was turning into an art project. Uncle Oscar would check in occasionally to help me through a particularly tricky aspect of the assembly but, for the most part, he left me alone.

School was drawing to a close, dandelions lined the path to the shop, and the boat was ready for paint. Red and white was the color scheme with the name "SANJI" painted in script down the center of the forward deck.

Launch was set for the coming tide on Saturday morning, the first day of summer vacation. That Friday, school was let out at noon and my first mission was to check to make sure the paint, applied just after midnight, was dry. Rounding the corner at the back of the barn my progress was arrested by an odd sight. The double doors at the front of the shop were ajar and a big moving truck with out-of-state plates was just pulling away from the parking lot at Mark's Garage.

With my heart practicing Olympic somersaults in my throat, I ran, as only a 16-year-old can, to the back door. My eyes took a second to adjust to the dim interior. The boat was gone! In its place was a huge flat object covered with brown packing blankets. Backing up in disbelief, my movements were suddenly impeded by an unseen object on the floor. There was an instant of arms and legs flailing then a crash that could be likened only to the sound of the Last Trump. A trap!

When the mind cleared and the fireworks stopped exploding inside my head, a strange sensation came over me. Alice, when she fell down the rabbit hole, must have felt much the same way. It was as though I was sitting in a boat. Closer investigation revealed, in fact, that I was sitting in a boat. The letters SANJI came into focus.

Regaining a somewhat vertical aspect and crossing to the large brown object as in a dream, my hand pulled back the blanket. Just above the keyboard were the words "Steinway and Sons."

It is unlikely that any of you have ever had the experience of spending the better part of a Maine winter building a nifty little outboard motorboat only to find on launch day that it had been moved to a dark corner of the shop and an enormous piano substituted in its place. It was the sort of thing that had never happened to me before either. Perplexed was the term. A trifle nonplussed would describe the case. One of my grandmother's homemade doughnuts seemed in order. These doughnuts had a clearing effect on the mind, and a clear mind would be needed to sort out this dilemma.

Through the screen door came the sound of voices raised in spirited conversation. One voice was recognizable as my grandmother's. The other would need a visual in order to place. That visual was not long in coming. Right in the middle of the kitchen floor my grandmother and Marianne Kneisel were toe to toe and things were starting to heat up. Anyone who knew either of these ladies would attest that they had strong personalities. My presence had a quieting effect. Mrs. Kneisel left and my grandmother went back to manufacturing doughnuts.

Every summer we all would take up residence in a temporary apartment in the back part of the house, just off the sun porch. The remainder of the living quarters was given over to the "students." My grandparents rented rooms to music students studying for the summer at Kneisel Hall. A lot of people did it. Took in students, I mean. A way to make a little extra cash. These students were collectively known around town as fiddlers. Most homes only had one or two, but we had at least a dozen or more. They would doss wherever space permitted. It would not surprise me if some of the most accomplished classical musicians of our time spent at least one summer at the old place.

My grandmother was very particular in that she would only accept female students and there was a strict rule that no young men were allowed in any of the rooms. I enjoyed a certain latitude in this respect, mostly because I lived there.

Back outside, sitting on the hood of the green Studebaker, a hot doughnut in each hand, the mystery began to unravel. Bits of the conversation started to make sense. The gist was that the piano had arrived and there was no room for it in the house. It was not part of the contract grandmother and Mrs. Kneisel had agreed to. Violins yes, cellos yes, even a bass viol was permissible. But, an unexpected honking big grand piano? That was pushing things. The men in the delivery van were determined to unload it and, rather than leave it in the driveway, it was "temporarily" shifted to the shop. And there it remained.

As scheduled, Rusty Duym and Mike Mackin showed up the next morning to assist with the launch. Stocking up on more doughnuts, we made our way to the shop. The resident piano was as much of a surprise to them as it had been to me.

Rusty inspected it carefully and wanted to know where you put the motor. Mike said that it looked as if it would leak and doubted if it could make it past the narrows.

It was a tight squeeze, but by tipping SANJI on her side, we were able to bring the boat into the fresh air of a June morning. It was the first time I had seen her outside the dingy light of the shop. The hull was painted white lead, a perfect contrast to the bright enamel red of the deck. The chrome cleats caught the sun's light and glittered like the Blue Hill Fair midway on Labor Day weekend. To me, that little boat was the most beautiful thing that ever could be imagined. The spell was broken by the sound of a young lady's voice. The accent was strange to me. "Hello, my name is Gena."

Like the moments just before a thunderstorm, a quiet sort of hush settled in the air around us. Rusty and Mike stood frozen in place, looking right past me in an awed sort of way, their jaws hanging somewhere around their third shirt buttons. One look in her direction was enough for me to revise my opinion that the boat was the most beautiful thing that ever could be imagined.

"Excuse me. Have you seen my piano?"

As you may remember, the month was June, the day was at the morning, the boat was ready for her launch, the piano was holding down the shop floor and the voice of Gena had stopped the flow of time for just under a moment and a half.

Mike looked at Rusty, Rusty looked at me, I looked at Gena and Gena looked through the open shop doors at her piano. The brown packing blankets still covered the instrument, but Gena made short work of removing them. Like a lieutenant at a dress inspection Gena went over every inch of Mr. Steinway's creation looking for any damage done by the moving company, or moving boats for that matter. She smiled, satisfied that all was well in the scratch-and-dent department.

Moving as one of the zephyrs that were playing about the tidewaters, Gena gently lifted the elegant mahogany cover, exposing eighty-eight keys of polished ebony and ivory. An eerie quiet settled about the four of us. Gena was in her own world. Her long fingers touched the keys and a sound such as Blue Hill had not heard before exploded like a cacophony of Angels.

As quickly as it had begun, the spell was broken. The music stopped and, like a vapor in the wind, Gena was gone.

Reason returned to her throne. There were things to do. Doughnuts to be eaten, boats to be launched, a summer to be lived.

Rusty and Mike took the stern and with self struggling with the bow cleat we made our way down over the grassy bank to Main Street. Traffic back then was not too much of an issue, but Ted Grindle, looking for all the world like Darth Vadar with his welding helmet tilted just above his eyes, came out of Mark's Garage and assisted in the crossing. At the time there was an alley of sorts between Rollie Howard's antique shop and Mark's Garage. It led to Mello's Wharf. Manuel Mello was Allen Mello's father and it was understood that Manuel had left his wharf to the town. All that remained of the wharf was old rotting pilings sticking out of the bank. There is nothing left of either the wharf or the alley today.

The tide was just coming full when three boys and a boat reached the water's edge. A launch is supposed to be a ceremony of sorts. Mike ran up to the pop machine at the garage and came back with a bottle of Coke. There was no way that a Coke bottle would break on the bow of a wooden boat so we just passed it around and drank it, like pirates drinking rum. SANJI slipped into the clear waters of the harbor and with a couple of pulls, the seven and a half horsepower Johnson came to life.

The inner harbor was flat calm. My fingers gripped the throttle and twisted. Tentatively the little boat moved forward and waves slapped against her sides. Another twist and the bow raised slightly, blocking my view ahead. The temptation was too great. Let's see what this baby will do! Full throttle!!! With the bow pointed toward Heaven we flew past the town wharf like a tomcat with something on its mind. Visibility was restricted by the candid position of the bow so it seemed prudent to climb up to the front in order to see what was ahead. The effect was instantaneous. The bow came down with a bang and the only part of the little boat that was still touching the water was the last inch or so. A fighter jet had nothing on us. Somewhere just east of the Big Rock we broke the sound barrier.

Easing off the throttle and giving the old heart a chance to get repositioned out of my throat and back in my chest were it belonged, SANJI compassed Johns Island and skipped like a spring lamb back toward Mello's Wharf.

The notes of a distant piano tinkled past my ears and splashed like crystals into the water beside the boat. It was a lovely morning. I wondered if Gena would care for a boat ride.

Gina, a student at Kneisel Hall, had materialized one June morning outside Uncle Oscar's workshop, the same workshop where over the previous winter the author had built a nifty little outboard motorboat. A Steinway grand piano now occupied the space where the boat had been. The boat launching was a success in part due to the background music. The seven and a half horsepower Johnson outboard performed as advertised, shooting the boat and me across the waves like an arrow from Cupid's bow.

Upon returning to Mello's Wharf the notes of the Steinway piano, now a permanent fixture of Uncle Oscar's shop, had drifted away into the afternoon air. When last seen, Gena was seated on the piano stool, looking like a model for a Sargent painting. The stool remained, but Gena was gone.

The tide was running out of the bay at a lively clip and it was in a similar fashion that I ran back to where the boat was tied. The channel of the little brook gave just enough depth that the boat floated into the center of the cove. Moored at the town wharf, SANJI spent the remainder of that afternoon cradled in the soft mudflats.

My thoughts turned back to the matter at hand—Gena. Stopping at the drugstore just long enough to place a nickel on the counter and order a root beer "frosty" allowed me time to think. Those who know the author have probably noticed that thinking is not one of his strongest points. However, the frosty had the magical effect of clearing the cobwebs from the old melon and allowed me to formulate a plan of action.

I had realized early on that in matters of being able to attract the opposite sex, Nature had not gone overboard on bestowing her favors on me. Nature had economized in the looks department as well as athletic ability. These two attributes, plus an access to a car, were what seemed to be uppermost in the qualities admired by the young ladies who then populated the halls of George Stevens Academy.

In matters of the heart, the only method that I found to have achieved results was persistence. It was this course of action that seemed prudent in my pursuit of Gena.

There was something different about Gena and it took a while for me to figure out what it was. First and foremost, she was a musician. Gena seemed to have no other interest in life except that cussed piano. With reams of sheet music propped up in front of her and that infernal metronome clicking away on top of the Steinway, she would practice the same thing over and over. Classically trained, she would sit at her piano for hours on end, practicing scales and strange sweeping movements that were probably actual songs.

It was at those times that opportunity presented itself. Sometimes a certain tool or a nail would require my entry into the interior of the shop where she was practicing. The first couple of times she ignored my presence. Then, though it was hard to believe, Gena would sometimes even seem annoyed by my interruptions, at one point actually asking me to leave.

The weeks passed and it began to look as though my plan was flawed. Persistence wasn't working as well as might be expected but, undaunted, I kept at it.

Hope was all but lost when around the middle of August the change came.

My visits to the shop were becoming much less frequent and for the last week or so they had ceased altogether.

It came as a shock to turn around one Thursday afternoon to find Gena standing at my elbow. She said she was part of a recital or something that was going on that evening at Kneisel Hall. She gave me a piece of paper that amounted to a ticket in and asked me to come.

The venue was sophisticated beyond anything this boy had ever encountered. The man in the black suit and bow tie at the door gave me a quick north-south and was about to say something when the paper that Gena had given me appeared in my hand. With a disgusted look he jerked his head and allowed me entry.

The doorman seemed to be the only one of the crowd who paid the least bit of attention to the "townie" with the green polyester shirt. There was a table set up with little triangular sandwiches and some funny tasting punch in a glass bowl. Fortified with food and a glass of punch I settled down at the back of the room to watch the proceedings.

By ones, twos, threes, fours and sometimes fives, the musicians took their turn. Melodies and notes soared and darted around the hall like a flock of barn swallows catching blackflies on a June morning. Gena was the last to play. There were two selections, one with a violin accompaniment, and the final, a solo. These two tunes were the only ones that evening that sounded familiar, as they were the very same that Gena had been practicing all summer. In a gown that looked to be a French designer original, Gena took her bow and applause supplanted the music.

The night air was mild with a breeze coming off the bay. Gena asked if I would walk her home. The request seemed odd because her Rambler was in the parking lot. At the time huge elm trees lined the street, creating a leafy corridor. For one of the first times in my life, words escaped me. We walked in silence. My only regret was that Kneisel Hall wasn't in Surry as the walk promised to be over much too soon for my liking.

Somehow we found ourselves on the old town wharf. Both the moon and the tide were close to full. My little boat bobbed at the side of the wharf. Gena looked at me and smiled.

It was latish the next morning before the author was roused out of bed by the sound of a loud knock and the words, "Are you going to sleep all day?" filtering through the woodwork.

Pulling on my clothes from the evening before and glancing at my watch further substantiated the lateness of the hour. The house was strangely quiet.

"Is Gena awake?" My query was met with a look of confusion.

"Gena went back to New York over a week ago."

The mists cleared from my adolescent mind. Was it all only a late summer night's dream?

Uncle Oscar had a pot of hours-old coffee on the stove. A cup seemed in order. My brain spun like a maelstrom. Gena was gone. The piano was gone. The summer was gone. A part of my youth was also gone.

Dragon Fire

There is a seminal time in a boy's life, somewhere between the ages of 7 and 13, when he grows from a child into a young man. It is not always an easy time and a good friend and companion is definitely an asset. God seemed to have designed the dog expressly for this purpose.

At 7, Fate stepped in, as She so often has in my life, and filled the bill. At my insistence, Pup was saved from the litter to be my dog.

It was a different time. Pup never had a collar or a leash and never needed one. We were both free to be young together.

A dog's way of thinking and a boy's way of thinking are very similar in many respects. Mother's favorite admonition was, "You know better than that!" It is arguable if either a boy of 7 or a dog of any age "knows better than that," but that is really not the point. Boys and dogs live in the moment. The consequences of any particular action are of little concern. We did things because they seemed a good idea at the time. The consequences sometimes were immediate but usually had to wait until somebody found out what you did. By then it was a different moment in which to live.

As they get older, boys learn from these consequences, dogs, not so much.

Water serves as a magnet for both dogs and boys. It was a summer morning with nothing of interest happening in Blue Hill village. Between Mark Clapp's garage and Alton Herrick's radio repair shop there was a small brook that ran over the property that now serves as the post office.

There was a large culvert that carried the brook under Main Street to the bay. The brook was but a trickle, and the culvert, long and dark, promised adventure. Pup in the lead, we followed the trickle into the inky depths. The culvert didn't seem very long when viewed from the street but the further in we got the darker and slipperier it became. We were entering a dragon's cave in search of treasure. Our footsteps echoed and the sound of our heartbeats reverberated off the steel corrugations.

The darkness surrounded us as a big truck rumbled over our heads. A truck? No! That was the terrible sound of an angry dragon in his lair.

Pup growled and there was no reasoning with him. His keen nose had picked up the dragon's traces and he was on them.

He was off into the darkness.

It was then that we encountered the dragon. The air was alive with dragons. Flapping dragon wings knocked me into the slimy water of the culvert floor. The dragon flew by me, hissing and breathing fire. Pup was in hot pursuit. Undaunted, he was setting up a din of his own.

It was a happy dog, a scared boy and a drake mallard that emerged back into the light that morning. Pup held his prize in his jaws. If ever a dog could smile, Pup was smiling. Annie Herrick, by contrast, wasn't. Alton and Annie kept a pen of tame ducks near the brook and the drake was a recent escapee.

Wrenching the bird from the jaws of death and uttering a few choice words in our direction, Annie went home to call my grandmother.

Now comes the worst part. My grandmother thought it would be the proper thing to do, to show our sincere regrets and concerns, if Pup and self would call on Annie that afternoon and inquire as to the wellbeing of father duck.

It may have been the only time in my memory when Grandmother was wrong. Even Pup could see the flaw in the plan—but we did as we were instructed.

The afternoon was already fairly warm, but shortly after my knock on Annie's door the temperature heated up considerably.

My practiced apology piece went by the wayside as the conversation was a bit one-sided.

Pup took the cue. In matters of dragons, his intelligence was undeniable. Seeing no reason to linger, we were across the yard and into the bushes in less than a moment.

Don't ask me about the duck's fate. If it did survive the culvert ordeal it would have probably expired of natural causes by now, anyway.

"Finast" Kind

When school was let out for summer recess, I was often packed off to spend a few days with my paternal grandparents in South Blue Hill. That part of town was known as the Neck. There were some nice homes on the Neck, but most of them were modest, even by the standards of the day, riches then being measured, not by gold, but in the coin of the spirit. Grammy Collins' house may have been modest on the outside, but the inside was so full of love that, to me, it seemed like a palace.

My left heel jacked the kickstand into flight position. A new pair of Red Ball Jets had the bike airborne with the first two turns of the pedals. Cutting through the Esso parking lot and touching down just long enough to run over the black rubber hose by the gas pumps sounded the bell and brought Cordell racing out of the grease bay, his face looking like an expectant pup who had just watched his master swallow the last bite of hot dog. Uncle Oscar looked up from the checkerboard carved in the top of the old wooden bench by the garage door and waved goodbye. I noticed this only because pilots have such great peripheral vision.

Reaching cruising altitude, crossing the Mill Brook, Blue Hill Bay opened up on my port side as MacIntire's market, the TA-CO restaurant and the department store flashed by on my starboard. Air space was congested at the Town Hall intersection but when the afterburners kicked in I was across Main Street in the blink of an eye.

"WARNING—WARNING" flashed on the cockpit console: civilian cargo carrier at eleven o'clock. Radar indicated it was Mrs. Obrien, my former second grade school teacher, exiting from the First National with two bags of groceries. Mrs. Obrien was one of my favorite teachers. Immediate evasive action was required or the FAA would have my license.

Nearly blacking out from the G forces, the bike pushed beyond its design limits; a midair disaster was narrowly averted. That fighter jet training had really paid off. Regaining control and banking smoothly past the library, the bike locked to a heading of due south down the Parker Point Road. Checking the cockpit indicated that the grocery bag containing my clothes was still secured in the bike's basket.

The grocery bag was emblazoned with the word "FINAST" in bold red letters. FINAST, the name of the store's product line, was an acronym for the first two letters of First National Stores. It came as an epiphany some time later when I realized this. It had made the difference between a C- and a D on a spelling test and the teacher was not impressed when I pointed out her error in grading by showing her the FINAST logo on an empty bag of potato chips that I had in my lunch box.

The First National, also known as the "chain store," was Blue Hill's first supermarket. It burned in a great fire when I was away at school, somewhere around the late mid '60s. Its prices were lower, but the smaller markets competed by extending credit to their customers. This was a godsend for some, particularly during the winter months when jobs were scarce and money was scarcer.

A certain gentleman of unreliable means was once called into the back office by the local market owner, his credit limit having been reached. With an almost apologetic tone in his voice, the owner began his oft-repeated plea. "Now, Joe, you know your bill is getting a mite high. Just what do you intend to do about it?"

There came a thoughtful reply. "I'll tell you what, Ben. I know you know I sometimes trade up at the chain store. So, if you agree to extend me more credit, you can have all my business."

"Finest kind" is an expression that, at the time, was not part of the common lexicon, but it certainly was descriptive of my elation that morning. Activating the autopilot, the twists and turns of Parker Point Road rolled effortlessly away, like that favorite shooter marble that I dropped the week before on the study hall floor.

Reaching the Falls Bridge the captain was met with trepidation. Sealed orders from Headquarters mandated that "Extreme Caution" be exercised in crossing the bridge. This was due to an incident, some many years previous, in the early days of aviation. Though the details are still classified, my understanding is that while coming down the hill in preparation for the bridge crossing, the front wheel of a certain misfortunate aviator's bicycle became detached from the whole and the resulting crash landing did the pilot a serious injury. This event had apparently made a grave impression on Grammy Collins' memory. Sealed orders were to walk my bike down the hill to the bridge and pedal up the other side, or, perhaps it was the opposite. The latter seemed more reasonable, as walking a bike down a perfectly good hill made no sense at all.

On closer inspection it became evident that this was no ordinary flight path. It was a diabolical test, put in the path of the wayward traveler by the people of the Neck, a test that only the bravest and most deserving might endeavor.

To pass, one must fly through a massive gate with concrete on the sides and top and a raging torrent below. The slightest miscalculation would mean disaster.

The aircraft, as if it was a living thing, seemed to sense the situation, nearly stalling for lack of airspeed.

"Airly Beacon" flashed as if burned into a cloud on my port side. What could it mean? It made no sense. It must be a code of the same sort encountered by Gandalf upon entering the mines of Moria. Frantically, my mind raced; the answer instantly revealed itself in its simplicity. Airly was to fly and beacon was the beacon of fearless truth.

Placing my fate in God's hands I pushed the throttle to maximum and nosed the aircraft into a steep dive. Timing was everything. Pinning the airspeed indicator, crossing the bridge and pulling back on the stick at precisely the right instant, I began my ascent, threading the needle and leaving behind the raging waters now even more enraged for my safe passage.

It was nearly dinner (noon) time as I brought the bike in for a perfect two-point landing on the specially constructed crushed-clamshell runway in front of Grammy's house. Climbing down from the cockpit the sight that met my eyes is as vivid as I write this as it was that day 50-odd years ago. The scene was set thus: Grandmother, perched like a chickadee on the top rung of a rickety wooden ladder, messing with an upstairs window. Lewis Henry, standing a respectful distance away, both hands in his pockets, peering heavenwards, his bottom jaw slightly ajar.

The conversation between the two ran as follows:

Lewis: "Gertie, what in the world are you doin' up top that ladder?"

Grammy: "Lewis, any darn fool can see I'm takin' off this storm window."

Lewis: "Gertie, a woman your age shouldn't be doin' that! Let me help!...Gertie, I'll steady the ladder!"

Aid and assist was my motto, but I was stymied as to how to help one's grandmother carry a storm window down a ladder. If only I had thought to bring my Buck Rogers jet pack.

Blueberries

Morning's at seven;
The hill-side's dew-pearled...
God's in his Heaven—
All's right with the world!

Robert Browning also included references to snails on
thorns and larks on the wing, but the thing that was clear was
that Pippa was in a good mood, or more likely putting up a good
front, the morning when she sprang from bed with that song on
her lips.

It was in a similar frame of mind the July morning found
me, with a blueberry rake in one hand, a half bushel basket in
the other, gazing down the length of the white strings, not to be
crossed, that defined the limits of my strip. It was my first day
of raking blueberries but destined not to be my last.

For those of you who have never experienced the joys of
raking blueberries, a slight amount of background is in order.

Money was a commodity that was always in short supply
and ways to attain it were even shorter. Raking berries was one
of the few options available for a young person to make some
cash for new school clothes and, of course, the Blue Hill Fair.

"Go talk to Forrest Closson, he might put you on." Uncle
Oscar's counsel was usually wise, and later that afternoon a
knock on Mr. Closson's door resulted in what amounted to my
first, and shortest, job interview. "So, you're Waldo's boy. Jim
Billings your grandfather? You willing to work?"

Wagging my head up and down like a toy dog in the back window of a '49 Plymouth was apparently taken as a reply in the affirmative. "Poker Valley, Monday morning, seven o'clock." Almost as an afterthought, "Sharp" was added just before he closed the door. He had also uttered phrases such as "second year berries" and "one-fifty a bushel," the meaning of which would surely be revealed in time.

There was a small kid-sized rake in the barn, but according to my grandmother, who seemed to be the resident expert on what the well-dressed blueberry raker required in way of apparel and accessories, a half bushel basket and a straw hat were absolutely essential. A $5 loan from Uncle Oscar provided the capital for the purchases. Merrill and Hinckley's carried the split ash basket while, just across Main Street, Sally's Variety stocked a line of straw sombreros with one of the nattier numbers being exactly my size.

It was outfitted thus that I arrived in Poker Valley. A glass jug of water and a couple of peanut butter and Marshmallow Fluff sandwiches rounded out the day's fare.

The blueberry operation is no doubt set up today much as it was then. The winnowing machine was located at a central point in the field. It was to this machine that one lugged the full baskets of berries. Pete Carter, the man who winnowed the berries, also kept a tally of how many bushels each person raked, and you were paid accordingly at the end of the week. The going rate was $1.50 a bushel and a good raker could rake 20 or more bushels a day, which was excellent money back then. Five bushels was a good day for me. It wasn't for lack of trying that found me short. Strength, endurance and technique, gained by years in the fields, separated the men from the boys.

About three weeks in, feeling in mid-season form, by day's end, seven, sometimes as many as eight, bushels would be marked on my tally sheet. Those were the days that would find me in bed right after supper, sore, sunburned, bug bitten and scratched up, closing my eyes and seeing nothing but blueberries until nature's sweet restorer brought lucid dreams of even more blueberries.

(That summer left a lasting impression. A wish to never see, or taste, another blueberry was foremost in my mind and that holds to this day. Surely, when I die, the Devil will put me to raking blueberries.)

There always seems to be one bad apple in every crowd. This particular apple's name was Trucker. What Nature had left out by way of brotherly love She had made up for in muscles, with the result that Trucker always raked at least one bushel more in a day than either my friend David or me. Like so many of the younger rakers, Trucker ate his share of blueberries during the day. This practice was frowned upon by the establishment, but, with a field full of beautiful blueberries, it was impossible to control.

It was the day that Trucker had upset the berries in David's basket that we had finally had enough. It was David who issued the challenge. "I've got fifty cents that says tomorrow I rake more berries than you do. Sage will even rake more berries than you do tomorrow. Are you in, Sage?"

Trucker laughed, not a nice laugh either, and the bet was on. Not knowing what was up, but knowing to trust David, I produced the two quarters.

To keep everything on the up and up, the monies were held by Pete the tallyman.

The following morning foretold another hot one. We had new strips and mine did not look promising, full of rocks and sweet ferns but none of the solid blue patches that made for easy picking. Resigned to the fact that my four bits was history, it was beginning to look like a far from spectacular day.

As was the morning custom, we were all standing around the winnowing machine, Trucker practicing some not so subtle taunting and David unwrapping a Milky Way candy bar. A candy bar was quite a novelty back then and it immediately caught Trucker's eye. David offered him a bite but Trucker guessed that he should have the whole thing. Neither David nor I was in a position to argue and Trucker devoured the Milky Way much the same way as a Labrador retriever devours a pork chop, barely pausing to chew but mentioning between swallows that he didn't know that they put peanuts in Milky Ways.

It was puzzling to me, too: peanuts in Milky Ways? When we were out of earshot David began laughing uncontrollably. Mocking Trucker, "I didn't know that they put peanuts in Milky Ways." Still not grasping the circs but knowing something big had gone down, so to speak, David choked back the laughter and the explanation continued.

"Peanuts! That big lummox thought they were peanuts."

After some moments, David regained enough composure to continue. "Ex-Lax."

I saw all.

Though the Ex-Lax had effectively nobbled the favorite, we both knew that there is no such thing as a sure thing. Raking as we had never raked before, we lugged basket after basket up to the winnowing machine where Pete appeared to be taking an active interest in our little flutter and reported the ongoing results. "You're down by two, David; three for you, Sage." It appeared that the rest of the crew was also beginning to take notice. It would not surprise me if Pete were making some book on his own.

Trucker spent the better part of the afternoon in the woods and the odds shifted in our favor. At 3:30 David and I collected the winnings. I kept my 50¢ and gave David the rest. He had certain expenses after all.

Trucker complained that he hadn't been feeling well. "Must have been something I ate."

"Yeah!" said Pete. "Blueberries!"

A Raft of Days

My friend David stood beside me on the old wharf behind the firehouse. It was a summer day that promised freedom, and we discussed how best to pass the rest of the afternoon. The tide was coming and we had spent the past quarter hour or so racing the tidewaters across the flats. My new sneakers were caked with primordial ooze and would never be the same. Sneakers held no notice for me, this pair had for only a passing moment in a boy's life.

The morning sun had done its job warming the mud flats. The cold Atlantic water was tempered to a point where it was bearable to boys 10 years and younger. Older folks, meaning people over 30, would not dream of swimming in the

ocean. As a matter of fact, it was interesting to note that most people over 30 could not swim at all. This included sailors and fishermen who spent much of their lives on the water.

David checked his Timex. It was a well-known scientific fact that if one went swimming within a half hour of eating a meal, one would be beset by cramps and drown. It had only been 20 minutes since we had both enjoyed a peanut butter and Marshmallow Fluff sandwich for lunch. The man who invented the peanut butter and marshmallow sandwich was a genius. The only way to improve on it is to make it with Skippy crunchy peanut butter and use Wonder Bread. Owing to jealousy on the part of a particular grandmother, there was no Wonder Bread to be found in our house. We were forced to make do with homemade yeast bread. The bread problem could be overcome, in part, by applying copious amounts of peanut butter and frosting the top slice with another layer of Marshmallow Fluff.

The ten-minute wait until the danger of cramps had passed took about an hour and a half in "Boy Time." Boy Time is similar to "Dog Years" in that time passes at a much slower rate for boys than it does for regular people. A five-day school week, for example, lasts approximately two months in Boy Time. The upside of this is that the summer recess from school stretches out to well over a year.

Channel 5, or perhaps Channel 2, had recently featured a Disney presentation of The Adventures of Tom Sawyer and Huckleberry Finn. The gist of the plot was quite straightforward: two boys drifting down a river on a raft, all the while having exciting things happen to them. The idea was considered from all sides and no flaw could be found. David said he would be Tom, leaving me to play the part of Huck. After closer examination we determined that one of the key elements was missing. We had no river. David, displaying his usual sagacity, thought that we could pretend that the ocean was a river and drift around on that. It did have a tide after all.

For the nonce, things looked pretty rosy. We had a great time planning our voyage, and the theme soon came to include the Captain Kidd motif. There was no reason not to believe that pirates once sailed the waters of Blue Hill Bay and that there wasn't buried pirate treasure on Sand Island.

After a swim out to the Big Rock, we decided to meet at the raft early the next morning. If we had been characters in a comic strip, the light bulbs floating over the top of our heads would have flashed on at the same time. A second flaw had been uncovered. We didn't have a raft.

Heck, how hard could it be to build a raft? If Tom Sawyer and Huck Finn could build one, there was no reason we couldn't.

To build a raft—a simple matter for two industrious young boys, or so it seemed in the beginning.

We repaired to Uncle Oscar's workshop where David made a list of the needed tools and materials while my time was spent with a #2 pencil, sketching out the blueprints on a scrap of lumber. It was understood, from the illustration in Mark Twain's book, that a raft about 25 feet long and 10 feet wide should fill the bill. The idea was to first construct the platform and later add a small cabin for overnight trips and extended voyages. A sea chest was to be included from the very beginning to store any buried pirate treasure that we would surely find.

There was a pile of old boards in the corner that would serve as a deck, and on the workbench we found two old hammers and a reasonable facsimile of a hand saw. David's list included nails. He had thought of everything. There were a few shortish nails in a drawer, but a vessel of this magnitude required big, long nails—in our opinion, the bigger and longer the better.

As with any project of this magnitude investment capital was required. We had a stash of a dozen or so empty pop bottles that could be redeemed at two cents per but that would not offset the entire financial outlay. By skillful negotiation, David extracted a quarter from one of the summer kids he knew in exchange for a six-bladed jackknife. Actually the jackknife had only one very dull blade. The contingent was fold-out spoons and forks and nail files. A visit to Uncle Oscar secured an advance on my next week's lawn-mowing bill.

Thus amply fortified with the ready, we visited Merrill and Hinckley's where a clerk led us to a back room stocked with wood barrels full of nails of every description. It was an epiphany to learn how many nails could be purchased for a dollar in those days. Given the large quantity of nails available we considered increasing the size of the raft in order not to waste any.

The necessary ingredients were assembled on the shore behind Mark Clapp's garage. The prandial hour was fast approaching and hunger was beginning to gnaw at our insides. Work of this magnitude could not be contemplated on an empty stomach. A glass of milk and a peanut butter and Marshmallow Fluff sandwich were just the stuff to give the troops. Such was to be had without question in my grandmother's kitchen, as long as we made our own and cleaned up afterwards.

Summer was coming in with the tide as we returned to the shore. All was in readiness save for the logs. Anyone knows that a raft has to have logs as a way to float the thing in the water. David checked his list of materials. Boards, yes. Nails, yes. Logs? Not there. We looked about us, and all the logs we saw were still standing upright. There were some nice trees and they were considered. Still it would be a lot of work and take precious time to cut down even one of the smaller elms.

David said that sometimes he had seen logs washed up along the shore, so a plan was struck to scour the coast. We walked along the east side of the harbor and were having no luck until we rounded the point by the cemetery. There, in a little cove, was a washed-up timber. It was well up toward the high water mark so we continued down toward Peters Cove. David spotted a tree that had fallen down over the bank. Someone had started to clean it up and had cut off the main trunk. It was a perfect raft log.

It was then that a deep voice from above asked us what we thought we were doing. The log apparently had an owner and this owner thought very highly of this particular log. The voice at first turned a deaf ear to our explanation until we came to the part about Tom Sawyer. The voice said he had read Tom Sawyer and Huckleberry Finn as a boy and he too had dreamed of building a raft but somehow never got around to it. The log was ours on the condition that if we were to sail by this way he would like a ride.

The next morning dawned warmish. There was a stillness in the air that promised good swimming. David was already working on getting the logs in place on the mud flats. We had found four, all told, and had floated them back on the incoming tide.

With blueprints in hand we started construction. The process was simple: nail the boards crossways on top of the logs. The boards served two purposes. First, they kept the logs together; and second, they made a nice deck. All the boards were too long so it was necessary to saw some of them off. Given that our saw was duller than a hoe, cutting a board to length was a slow and exhausting process that got slower and more exhausting as the sun made her way skyward. Uneven boards, it was decided, would add a bit of a contemporary flair to her lines.

Work continued at a fairly rapid rate until the bell in the village clock struck twelve. The peanut butter and Marshmallow Fluff sandwich motif from the day before was repeated. And it was with full tummies and light hearts that we headed back to the shore. It has been said that all great minds think as one, and so it was with us. What our raft needed, particularly for extended voyages in search of pirate treasure, was a sail. Ancient mariners paid close attention to omens, and there staring us in the face was the mother of all omens.

This was laundry day, and right in front of us were three or four white cotton sheets hanging on the clothesline. Not only that, but a perfect mast was propped under the middle of one of the lines to keep it from sagging.

There were lots of sheets and nobody would even notice if we borrowed just one. And as far as the mast, that was just an old stick.

We had our sail and with a couple of nails secured the mast to the deck. The tide was full and all that was needed for a perfect launch was a bottle of champagne. David had a nickel left over from the nail purchase, just enough for a bottle of pop from the Coke machine at the garage.

Rather than waste the whole bottle on the christening we drank almost all of it and shook up what was left, and after we had argued about which end was the bow, sprayed both ends just to be sure.

It was on an ebbing tide that we made the Huck Finn's maiden voyage.

For readers who are not familiar with the tides in Blue Hill Harbor, an explanation is in order. The tide comes in and then the tide goes out. These events repeat themselves twice every day, although not always at the same time. The other interesting thing is that when the tide is in, the harbor is full of water. When the tide is out, it isn't. Instead of water, there are mud flats. That's how it was and that's how it still is today.

Our little raft was a huge success. Between the outgoing tide and an offshore breeze we were making great headway. Hub Island passed on our port side and we were pointing for the Big Rock.

We drifted even further and David said it might be a good idea if we could turn around before we got too far out. With all good intentions we agreed to head back to port. Good intentions, though, weren't any help at all. Things were looking bleak as we continued our outward passage. Johns Island was on our starboard at about thirty yards distant. It looked like it was an easy swim and it seemed the only option.

David went in first and made for the ledge off the west side of the island. It was an Olympic stroke, the Australian crawl, that proved most efficacious. That thirty yards proved more difficult than expected and if not for the assistance of my Guardian Angel (who once worked for Moses) parting the waves as I passed, this story might have had a different ending.

David and self sat shivering on the barnacle-encrusted ledge waiting for the tide to finish its day's work. Our raft was still on course, headed for the Narrows and then, no doubt, Spain.

It was suppertime before the water had lowered to a point sufficient for us to walk back to shore.

Blackened with mud and red from the sun, David said we could look for the raft in the morning, but we both knew we would never see it again.

It was a slow walk back to the house. What waited for me would not be pleasant but hey, how often do you get to have a raft like that?

Little Green App

My grandmother often s

would provide" and it seemed that sometimes He did a better
job than others. In the fun department, He often outdid
himself, particularly in the early summer.

Our fun did not come with a price tag; most of the time it
was free. It was not found in a videogame or even a special toy.
It was found in our imaginations.

It just so happened that we had hens. These hens had a
henhouse. This henhouse had a fairly flat roof. It was strictly
forbidden for young boys to climb up on the henhouse roof. The
reason for this particular rule still remains unclear to me but,
be that as it may, it was settled law. "No boys allowed on the
henhouse roof."

Behind the henhouse was an ancient apple tree. Its limbs
spread out over the hen pen and more importantly, over the
henhouse roof.

A Monday morning, early on in summer vacation, found
two boys sitting on the highest part of the henhouse roof. The
day was both young and pleasant and the breeze off the bay
blew in as much free fun as we could handle.

What to do? Together we had 15 cents, enough for two
small ice cream cones at the TA-CO restaurant. David thought
it best to save the ice cream cones until the afternoon, when it
was hotter. The motion passed.

That was fun. What next? The thing is that young boys

om men and older boys. Older boys would tell you
gs; men, you had to watch and listen to.

David took out his Kamp King jackknife. "Look what Steve
showed me." Steve was in the eighth grade. From the apple tree
David cut a long slender branch and pruned it until it resembled
a stick for cooking marshmallows. Picking a little green
apple, David stuck it on the end of the stick. Still, much like
a marshmallow roast. Here is where David diverted from the
motif. With a sharp flick of the wrist, he flung that little green
apple high into the air.

No Kamp King for me, but Uncle Oscar had taught me how
to sharpen an old knife he had given me. This was a standard
issue jackknife with two blades. The big blade was for utilitarian
matters. The little blade was the sharp blade.

Whittling and pointing out produced a near clone of
David's throwing stick, and before long we mastered both
accuracy and distance.

Napoleon could not have fortified a more strategic position
than that henhouse roof. An opening between Uncle Oscar's shop
and the barn provided direct access to Main Street. A dump truck
drove past. Splat, splat, two apples found their mark.

After each throw we would flatten ourselves against the
roof and wait for the all clear. It wasn't until, by an error in
"windage," I managed to place my apple through the open
window of a '47 Dodge sedan that the realization came that the
morning's fun was about to end.

Grandmother's voice could be heard in the backyard with
its tone not unlike that of the last trump. The rest of the story
is too painful to tell, but as sure as God made little green apples,
we had fun while it lasted.

Popcorn

Toward the last couple weeks in August one began to notice changes at the Blue Hill Fairgrounds. The concession tents and the rides popped up during the day like mushrooms after a rain. Most evenings after supper, my grandmother would want to see the latest developments. We all piled into the old green Studebaker, the model that looked the same coming and going, and headed up Greene's Hill. Dust and diesel hung in the air, games of chance lined both sides of the midway and the colored lights of the rides blinked on at dusk. For a boy it was the most wonderful time imaginable.

As Labor Day weekend approached, the activity at the fairgrounds increased at an exponential rate. Saturday was the day the fair opened and it was my goal to squeeze in every hour that was humanly possible. Every minute within the hallowed confines of the Fairgrounds was worth a dozen on the outside.

As with all good things, this plan had a downside. Our family had a permanent concession stand, a white building with a flat roof that sold popcorn and chocolate-dipped ice cream on a stick. Upon my reaching a certain age, Uncle Oscar called me into service, peddling popcorn in the grandstand. On Sunday afternoons the Fair would feature "Norm Lambert at the Electric Hammond Organ." Norm would occupy center stage in front of the grandstand and smile. I never cared for his music, but could he ever smile. It was said that his smile would charm the porcupines out from under the judges' stand.

Old ladies, tired from walking up and down the midway, would drag their unfortunate husbands up to the grandstand to see Norm Lambert smile. Armed with boxes of popcorn and a nail apron filled with change, I would walk up and down the isles of the grandstand yelling "Popcorn!" at the top of my lungs. This had a tendency to annoy Norm, who would sometimes misplace his ubiquitous smile and stare daggers at me from across the track. From a selling standpoint, the technique worked. People soon learned that the yelling stopped when a sale was being made and buying a box of popcorn was a sure way to shut me up. Twenty cents seemed like a good deal.

Saturday night was my favorite. It was the night that featured the "World Famous Hell Drivers." If you wanted a seat for the performance you had to get there early. The grandstand was always filled to capacity. As a professional popcorn vendor

I had free admission to any and all performances. It tried my young voice to be heard over the din of the high performance automobiles as they rocketed up and down the racetrack. It was only at times when there was a break in the performance or when the clown was relating the slightly off-color joke about hunting polar bears, that popcorn sales were possible. Early in my career I learned that the popcorn business is fickle. Some nights you couldn't give a box away, other times there wasn't enough popcorn in Hancock County to supply the demand.

It was the latter circumstance that prevailed on the night in question. The Hell Drivers were tearing up the racetrack with more noise than usual, the clown was demonstrating how to kick a polar bear, and popcorn futures were through the roof. Uncle Oscar was manufacturing the stuff as fast as the machine could produce it and I ran back and forth from the grandstand, stopping just long enough to empty my nail apron of money and to get a fresh supply of corn.

About half way through the performance, an odd thing happened. As you may remember, the price for a box of popcorn was twenty cents. Most people gave me a quarter. That called for a nickel in change. In time, it reached a point where there were no nickels left in my nail apron. It was certainly a dilemma. I was out of business. A man to my left wanted popcorn and gave me a quarter. I handed him the popcorn and explained that I could not make change. He was noticeably upset. What to do? Like the stunt cars on the racetrack, my mind went into overdrive. I thrust another box of popcorn toward him; seeing his angry countenance replaced by a broad grin told me that the problem was solved. The rest of the show there was a "two for a quarter" sale on popcorn.

After the fair shut down the family gathered around my grandmother's kitchen table and made an accounting of the day's receipts. My grandmother, the official bookkeeper, announced that the day's popcorn sales had surpassed all previous records. My story of the events on the grandstand was met with mixed reviews. There was one male family member who strongly disapproved of my independent actions and made no attempt to keep his opinion to himself, elevating vituperation to an art form.

It was a tired, broken-spirited little boy who met Uncle Oscar in the dim hallway outside my room. Laying a hand on my shoulder, his smile lit up the passage.

"You did great!"

Fair Time

Oh! Do not attack me with your watch.
A watch is always too fast or too slow.
I cannot be dictated to by a watch.

—Jane Austen

Blue Hill Fair takes place on Labor Day weekend, and has for as long as anyone can remember. The Fair is a landmark in time, the traditional end of summer. For a boy, it marked the transition between summer vacation and the new school year. One last hurrah, the Fair was a time to exult in the sheer joy of being young; to have the freedom afforded by the anonymity of the crowds on the midway and the luxury of spending money in an atmosphere of the completely frivolous and over-priced. Summer vacation had gone on forever and the infinity of the school year loomed ahead. Time, that elusive master that now runs our lives and pushes us along in its ever-faster current, in youth but circled about us, as though we were caught in an eddy at the river's edge.

Uncle Oscar had a concession stand at the Fair near the north end of the bleachers, a permanent structure, white, with a flat roof. Most of the year it stood boarded up, but as Labor Day weekend approached it became the center of activity. It was a family venture with popcorn, ice cream sandwiches and my grandmother's homemade doughnuts. The idea was to make enough money to pay the property taxes.

The Fair produced a microcosm of people: the fortune-telling Gypsies in their new Cadillac, the farmers from all over the state who brought their livestock to exhibit and often slept in the same stalls, the blind accordion player who would play for hours for donations he received in an open wooden cigar box; the tattooed carnies, the horsemen who lived for their animals and spoke of little but harness racing, and the everyday people who walked and re-walked the dusty midway that stretched between the girlie show tent and the King and Queen French Fry trailer.

It was the year with the exhibit featuring the world's largest pig. For a mere twenty-five cents, one could view a sow that was so fat as to be hardly able to stand under her own weight. Coming away from the exhibit with a slightly uneasy feeling and trying to sort it all out in my young mind, my attention was arrested by a golden flash from one of the many games of chance that lined the midway. Drawing me as if by a magic spell, the source of the flash was soon revealed: a solid gold pocket watch, the sort of watch that rich people wore. It even had a matching gold fob. I wanted that watch, and the only way to acquire it was to win it.

The barker saw me eying his stall and waved me over. It was an odd sort of game, set up like a flat roulette wheel with brightly colored numbered holes around the perimeter. The wheel was set spinning and a white mouse was released in the center. The mouse, in a state of bewildered confusion, would scamper about and finally jump down one of the holes. To win, you and the mouse had to agree on the same hole. Each win would produce a coupon. The cheap prizes could be had for one or two coupons, but the gold watch...

Laying down a quarter and picking the hole that was painted black, thinking that it would attract the mouse, I won the first game, a good omen.

Playing the game whenever availed of both opportunity and funds, watching the little mouse as he dizzily staggered about the board, my coupons began to increase in number. By Labor Day evening, realizing that time—along with my supply of quarters—was running out, panic fell over me like a toad beneath the harrow. Sheer desperation found me in the concession stand. Uncle Oscar was popping corn. Somehow he knew what I was about and, without a word, he drew four quarters from the till. Taking his own watch from his pocket he glanced at the time. "You had better hurry, they'll be closing up soon."

Panic overcame me. "What time is it?" I blurted, glancing at the old watch in his hand for reassurance. Under the bright lights of the midway something seemed amiss. Uncle Oscar's watch had only one hand.

At the stall, the four quarters disappeared in the blink of an eye. Standing alone, three coupons short, in the now-darkening midway, watching the barker lower the flaps on his tent, I saw the midway start to blur and the colored lights run together like watercolors on an artist's pallet.

"What you got there?" he asked, pulling the coupons from my numb fingers. Tearing the coupons in two and throwing them on the floor of the tent he removed the watch from its place of honor and handed it to me. Standing alone with my treasure, my unheard "thank you" floated down the now-dark midway and mingled with the smell of cotton candy as the final tent flap closed with a bang.

As it turned out, the watch was not gold after all. It broke the second time I wound it. I kept it for a while, but finally ended up swapping it with David for an old rusty jackknife.

A few Christmases ago while opening my allotment of socks and plaid work shirts, a small package found its way to my chair. Inside, wrapped in white tissue paper, was Uncle Oscar's watch. Mom had found it while going through some family things, and remembering my fascination for the watch with one hand, had given it to me for Christmas.

Time was frozen forever on its face, somewhere between eleven and twelve o'clock.

The Round Button

"**It must have** been the clams."

Lewis's logic, though undoubtedly correct, was sometimes hard to follow. His mind worked differently than most; rather than jumping to conclusions, he jumped over them.

But, I am getting ahead of myself. It was not in the so distant past that even those with the meanest of intelligence would understand the phrase "turning the button." Today, the once ubiquitous button to which I refer has fallen from use, although it is far from extinct. If the reader is unfamiliar with the term, read on; all will be revealed.

I was fortunate as a child to be part of a tradition that has nearly vanished from the landscape. Before the days of on-demand movies, or televisions for that matter, folks provided their own entertainment. Often on Saturday evenings, after the traditional supper of baked beans and yeast rolls, we would all sit around my grandparents' living room and the grownups would swap stories. It was like the old "Bert and I" records of the '60s, except that this was the real Tabasco.

My aunt Helen, a published authoress I might add, advised me that parts of this story might not be entirely factual. Having heard it told countless times, I have no doubt of the story's veracity, but, never argue with an aunt is my motto. I am, after all, but the chronicler.

The winter gales, followed by the August heat, had taken their toll. Everyone knew what had to be done, but a change such as this requires careful consideration and planning. As the breakfast bacon sizzled in the cast iron spider and the sliced yeast bread toasted on the covers of the old kitchen stove, the pros and cons of a new outhouse were discussed. There was a strong argument for keeping the old outhouse, as such a place cannot help but harbor a sort of sentimental attachment, but, in the end, cool heads prevailed.

Ellen noted that the seat had cracked, a painful situation, the roof leaked, one of the floor boards was missing and the original architect had positioned the structure so that the north wind blew snow up through the seat. One could live with these minor inconveniences, but the scales were tipped by the fact that the old place had seen a lot of use and the chances of it fulfilling its duties for another long Maine winter were remote.

The decision being made, Lewis and his father Oren sprang to action. To paraphrase Steinbeck's remark about Doc and the boys, only two lazier men could have accomplished more in so short a time, and by suppertime the new building was completed. To conserve materials, the door from the old outhouse was hung on the new privy. A slight deviation from plumb caused the door to swing open. Oren picked up his claw hammer and set to removing the old button. Lewis stopped him short. "This has to be the finest outhouse on the neck. We can't use that old button. I'll make us a new one."

For those of you not familiar with the term, a button was a necessary part of an outhouse, an inexpensive and rather ingenious device consisting of a rectangular block of wood nailed in such a way as to allow the door to open when in the vertical position and to hold it closed when in the horizontal position.

Retrieving a bucksaw from the woodshed, Lewis sliced about an inch off the end of a beautiful stick of white birch firewood. Admiring his handiwork in the slanted rays of the afternoon sun a smile cracked the weathered features of his ageless face. "We'll have the only round button on the neck."

A 16-penny nail driven through the precise center fixed the new button at exactly the right height. Oren, clearly overcome by the majesty of the situation, was drawn, as a man in a trance, toward the new button. He and Lewis took turns working it until it spun as freely as a wheel on an upside-down bicycle. Both admitted its beauty was unsurpassed.

Christening a new outhouse was as important as launching a boat. Ellen volunteered. Turning the new button failed to produce results. No matter how she spun the button the door wouldn't open.

As if on cue, the dull gray clouds of that October evening cast a pall that reflected in the forlorn faces of the assembled. For what seemed an eternity, silence reigned, broken only by the wind as it backed into the north.

At length, with the glittering light of intelligence radiating from every pore, Lewis gave tongue. "Dad, we are a couple of darn fools! That door will never open like that! Anyone can see the problem! We nailed the button to the doorframe. We should have nailed it to the door."

Puppy Love

For reasons unexplained, one winter my parents consented to dog-sit a pureblood cocker spaniel. Lady was the animal's name. You may remember Lady and the Tramp? Well, the Disney Studios could have camped out on our doorstep for movie material. Our Tramp's real name was Blackie, a beautiful black lab belonging to Roy and Madeline Snow who lived across the street.

It was a movie romance in many respects. Every male dog between Sedgwick and Surry was entrenched in our yard for two weeks as Lady plied her doggie wiles among the many-legged.

Disputes between the suitors were common and fights would break out at all hours of the day and night. Many a morning I would look out, expecting to see dog parts scattered across the dooryard, but the fights consisted mostly of "sound and fury, signifying nothing." Shakespeare must have understood dogs.

Try as they might, my parents could not repeal the laws of Nature. Eventually, Lady needed to go "out" and when she did there was a small army of dogs waiting, as patience on a moment, for the adored one to appear. Not being old enough to understand exactly was happening in dogland, the whole matter continued a mystery. Questions to adults who should know brought reluctant answers that indicated they had no idea either.

The result was that some weeks later, behind the kitchen stove, Lady produced a sizeable litter of puppies. They were a cute loveable bunch of assorted pedigrees. One little black fellow, who looked like the majestic Blackie, took a natural liking to me and I to him. As he grew older he needed a name and "the pup" got shortened to Pup. Mom and Dad said I could keep one of the litter, and Pup was the one.

It was nearly spring when Lady's owners came to collect her. The resulting scene made quite an impression on my young mind. Hiding in the entry, the best place for a hasty departure if things got really bad, I was witness to the unfolding drama taking place in the kitchen. The problem, other than the obvious matter of the dozen or so puppies, was the owner's realization that since being remanded to our care, Lady had neither been bathed nor clipped. To add insult to injury, Lady had obviously been bred to a dog or dogs of questionable spaniel lineage pedigree.

The discussion in the kitchen grew louder and more animated by the minute. There was an obvious disagreement between the parties and accusations were flying around like baseballs at a Little League game.

One advantage in being young is that, by necessity, you are also small. This fact proved a benefit as I squeezed behind the door as our guests, replete with Lady and family, exited the premises like a great rushing wind.

How long I remained hidden is uncertain, but all was quiet on the home front when I finally had the nerve to make my way back into the kitchen.

An eerie silence pervaded the room. Even Lady's dog bed was gone. A kitchen without a dog sleeping next to the stove is a sad thing, and gloom settled over me like fog on a pebble. My thoughts in times of despair often turned to ice cream and, remembering that there might be some left of a quart of Sealtest harlequin, my attention, as well as my feet, wandered to the Kelvinator that lived in the far corner. The ice cream was gone.

In the mounting silence that sings to grief, a small glad sound came from behind the wood box. Closer investigation revealed its source. A little black shape was huddled in the shadows. Both the puppy and I were shaking as I gently lifted him into the light. As Ariadne had fallen asleep and been left behind by Theseus on the Isle of Crete, so had Pup been left behind in our kitchen.

Pup was afraid that the scary people might come back for him so we decided to hide. Under the quilt at the foot of my bed seemed the perfect place.

That night, and for many years thereafter, my feet were warmed by the love of a true friend.

"Five, six, pick up sticks; seven, eight, lay them straight"

The morning sun revealed an unfamiliar mountain in the driveway. Where it came from is lost in the vales of time. The salient point was that the space where Grandmother normally parked her green Studebaker was now occupied by about ten cords of firewood. Maine firewood comes in "sticks," not "logs," and there looked to be thousands of sticks of the stuff.

A glance up the driveway revealed that the Studebaker was not buried beneath the woodpile. It was, however, blocked in next to the barn and looked as if it had little or no chance of cruising the streets of Blue Hill until sometime next spring. Grandmother was fond of her Studebaker and even more fond of her weekly trip to Newberry's five and dime in Ellsworth. My suspicion was that the Studebaker would not be out of circulation for long.

The wood had been late in arriving and a similar remark was said of me. Since reaching boy's estate it was my policy to spend as much time on Saturday mornings snuggled beneath the counterpane as possible. There was mention that today was "wood day'" and my stated intention had been to rest up in preparation for the work ahead. Uncle Oscar looked knowingly across the breakfast table, giving no credit to my explanation.

Wood was the only form of heat in the old house. There was a wood furnace in the cellar and a parlor stove, or heater, in the ell. A large floor register was located in the hall directly above the furnace. This register was about the size of a kitchen table and ideally positioned to heat the main house. Even when the mercury stayed around zero for weeks at a stretch, the house was never cold.

The firewood in the driveway was destined to be stored in the cellar and it was to this end that the day's labors would be devoted. Putting up the winter firewood was a ritual that had been repeated every fall for generations and that day found representatives of the last three, shedding jackets and donning gloves.

The glass sash had been removed and was safely placed on the piazza. The opening into the cellar was small and careful aim was required to throw the stick in without hitting the wooden frame. The frame around the cellar window was worn and had doubtless been replaced many times, but one could still draw rebuke with a direct hit.

Instinctively we set up a sort of assembly line, taking turns and firing the sticks through the opening like some sort of many-handed machine.

In a short time there was no room left to throw and everyone went down cellar to stack. Neat rows of evenly laid wood formed against the massive granite foundation stones, row on row, until it seemed as though there would not be room for it all.

The shorter pieces of wood destined for the parlor heater had their own place over by the cistern. My tiers were not as uniform, but slowly the art of stacking wood was learned and still serves me well.

The Studebaker was liberated shortly before dark. The first fire of the season burned in the parlor stove. Grandmother had supper ready, hot chicken with rice soup. Its nourishing warmth seemed to hit the spot. The muscles were tired, the good kind of tired that comes from honest work and a sense of accomplishment.

Of the many generations that spent a Saturday putting up a winter's wood in the old place, it turned out that that boy would be the last.

The following spring the old wood furnace was replaced by a shiny new one that burned oil. The house was still warm, but it was never quite the same.

Things Go By

One of my earlier memories was of the family moving from our little house on the "Acre" to the old Stover farm on South Street.

At the time, South Street was a dirt road, and the old Stover farmhouse, one of the oldest in town, was quite a set of buildings. We had just settled in when the house caught fire and burned flat. No one was hurt, but all that was left of the old place when I next saw it was a smoldering cellar hole. The henhouse and barn were still standing. The reason the barn was spared was a sufficient separation from the house and the west wind that took the flames away. The saving of the henhouse could not be attributed to its location or for any other reason that anyone could see. It amounted to a modern-day miracle.

Over time, the main house was rebuilt on a much less grand scale, and the henhouse and the old barn stood proudly vacant against the green fields. The barn was a great place for a boy to play. Its usefulness had long passed, but it was full of ghosts and unremembered memories. It was also full of barn swallows.

Some folks can see any bird and tell you what sort it is. My bird recognition is not on a par with that. My confidence abounds in identifying seagulls and robins. Crows are right up there, too; however there is some uncertainty regarding the distinction between a crow and a raven. If a crow were in a row of corn, and cocked his head and uttered "Nevermore," one would assume it was not a crow, but rather a raven, though one would be hard pressed to believe him.

The barn swallow is one bird that I can recognize without doubt. Every spring they returned from wherever they wintered and took up residence in the old barn. Bird access was easy, for the slider on the big door was rusted open and most of the windows were broken. Both wind and swallows found a home in the old barn.

From a boy's perspective, the barn swallow's sole purpose was to catch flying bugs. It was particularly adept at catching blackflies. We had more than our share of blackflies and many a spring morning, with his own personal squadron of barn swallows in tow, this author would walk down through the field to the trout brook. It was a symbiotic relationship. In quest of breakfast, the blackflies would swarm around me. Barn swallows would dive-bomb within inches of my head, making their own breakfast of the little black devils. Having already had my breakfast, I was looking forward to brook trout, rolled in flour and fried in bacon fat for lunch.

The barn stood abandoned for a few years. One fall, Dad decided to tear it down. The old boards, some twenty inches wide, were removed and stacked for future use. All that remained was the bare skeleton standing like a specter against the clear October sky.

The following afternoon Dad arrived home from work with a borrowed dump truck and a length of steel cable. An assortment of neighbors had assembled to watch the proceedings. The cable was secured to the barn's topmost ridge beam and the near end was hooked to the back of the dump truck. I was instructed to stand way back.

Dad remarked that all that was needed now was a little tug and the frame would fall like matchsticks. Cy Piper said he was not so sure. His remarks went unheeded.

With Dad in the pilot's seat, the dump truck was placed in a strong gear and the slack came out of the cable. The motor strained and the cable tightened until it sang in the wind like violin string. The old barn stood against the onslaught until the dump truck sputtered and died. The hand-hewn barn beams were mortised and pegged. That barn had been built to last.

In the failing daylight, one could see the shades of old, the farmers who had raised her one summer day, some hundred years past. If nothing else, they could take pride in their work. The barn fought a valiant fight, but in the end it was not equal to dump trucks and chainsaws. When at last she knew she had been beaten there was a crack like a rifle shot, followed by the moan of riven timbers, culminating in a cacophony of broken splinters. The dust of centuries rose like a cloud toward Heaven and was borne away, along with the shades, into the October sunset.

Spring followed winter, and one morning the brook called. Donning fishing rod and angleworms I set off down though the damp field grasses. The blackflies were as thick as blazes and I looked about for the swallows. They had returned and fifty or more were circling the spot where the barn had once been. The birds seemed confused. They didn't understand what had happened. Come to think of it, neither did I.

The Devil's Fiddle

The snare was set.

The back of *True* magazine had a section of classified ads and one was for a book, which could be had for the sum of 25 cents plus postage, on ghosts—real, scary ghosts. When it arrived, after what seemed an eternity, it turned out to be not what one would call a real book, more like a tract or pamphlet, but it did the trick. David and I studied it and after we had the stories memorized we told Trucker he couldn't read it. Trucker then proceeded to take it away from us.

Whenever Trucker was around, David would bring the conversation to ghosts. There is a principle called "the hundredth monkey," which says that if you tell someone something enough times, after a while, they will believe it.

Within a month Trucker believed in ghosts.

"Devil's Fiddle" is the common name. It was Uncle Oscar who had, in passing, mentioned the nefarious noise-making apparatus. When he was a boy, Uncle Oscar said he had used one to revenge a wrong that he suffered from an overly strict schoolmaster. It was a delightful story that any boy could appreciate, and David and I could not wait to try one out, Halloween being the perfect night.

The first step was for us to swear an oath of secrecy, the second to find the materials needed for its construction. These materials had to be expendable, so outright purchase was out of the question. We found everything we required hanging on a wooden peg in my grandfather's barn.

The weeks before Halloween dragged, but the big night finally arrived.

The choice of costumes was important. Ghosts were out of the question, too visible. A hobo with a slouch hat and a dirty face was David's choice; a pirate, mine.

It meant a sacrifice on our part. It was a long walk to Trucker's house. We had an official Boy Scout lantern supplied with fresh Eveready batteries, but we dared not to use it for fear of being seen. The darkness of that Halloween night covered us with an icy blanket. Every sound echoed in our ears and shadows took on eerie forms. It was a scene from Disney's Legend of Sleepy Hollow, ragged clouds racing past the gibbous moon while the bare branches of the old elm tree assumed demonic shapes with gnarled hands grabbing at the wind.

Shivering in the darkness, realizing that there might be something to this Halloween stuff, I glanced at David. He returned the "is it worth it?" look. Stoic, we both knew that it was. The luminous hands of my Timex wristwatch, a birthday present from my Uncle Harvard, read 11:45. The pirate costume was of little value in rapidly falling temperatures. Was it necessary to wait until exactly midnight on All Hallows Eve? As any pirate will tell you, timing is everything.

At 11:55, taking the mackerel jig in hand, the pirate crept silently to Trucker's bedroom window. The fishhook was securely fastened to the middle of the lower window sash. Fathom after fathom of line was let out until sanctuary was reached at the edge of the woods.

This was the moment of truth. In a sawing motion, rosin from an ancient spruce tree was gently drawn back and forth on the taut mackerel line. At first nothing happened, then, as if called up from below, the sound. It started as a low groan but with practice, tightening the line, the groan became a wail. The old glass window sang like a soprano in the Devil's opera. Trucker's nightmares of ghosts were realized and his voice joined in the chorus.

David and I took turns composing on the mackerel line until our concert was interrupted by the sound of the back door slamming and a lawn full of flashlights.

Like specters, we vanished into the night.

A Quiet Birthday

It was the morning of November 19. This may have little significance to you but to me it was a big deal. It just so happens that November 19 is my birthday, and this particular November was what one might call a milestone on the railway of life.

The year was 1958. It was an interesting year. Pope Pius pronounced St. Clare the patron saint of television. Sputnik, a satellite that the Russians had bunged into space the previous year had, as most suspected, come crashing back down to earth. Sputnik looked like a basketball porcupined with automobile antennae salvaged from old Buicks. Its purpose was to orbit the planet making beeping noises.

Not to be outdone, the U.S. had launched its own version, the Explorer. Leave it to our government to come up with catchy names. The nightly news explained that the Explorer version was far superior to Sputnik in that it had an FM radio. In 1958, about the only thing on FM was opera and I saw no advantage.

Atomic bombs were all the rage. Both the United States and Russia were lighting off atomic bombs on a weekly basis. One of our bombers dropped one by mistake on a house somewhere in South Carolina. Nobody was home at the time and it only partly exploded. Sort of a "good news, bad news" thing. They also lost an H-bomb in the ocean off Savannah, Georgia. That one might still be there, for all I know.

But I digress. On this particular November 19, I was

turning 11 years old. The inevitability of the fact could not be denied. Up until now I could put the thing off as something that was well in the future, but on that morning there was no getting around it—my 11th birthday had arrived.

Previous birthdays had been a good thing, but this one was different and had to be dealt with. The problem was that Marnie, my grandmother, had always said that when I was 11 my voice would "crack" or "break." It was the simple trust of an 11-year-old for me to believe that the transformation would happen precisely on my 11th birthday. This occurrence would somehow signal my "change" toward manhood. She was not specific what this change would be, but the fact was that I was quite happy with the present situation and from what I had seen of manhood it would be a good idea to put it off as long as possible.

I must have fallen asleep with the radio on for it was still tuned to WMEX in Boston and sounds of Johnny B. Goode filled the room when I awoke. It was still dark outside as I made my way down the hall passage. A flip of the switch in the bathroom brought the fluorescent fixture to life, flashing a few times in a psychedelic sort of way and then getting down to the business of casting a cold bluish glow about the small room. It was all there, neatly laid out, in the medicine cabinet. Man stuff. A Gillette safety razor with a new pack of "Gillette Blue Blades," a shaving brush in its own little cup, a bottle of Aqua Velva and next to that an amber bottle of Vitalis. Removing the cap from the Aqua Velva bottle and taking a whiff cemented my resolve. No voice cracking for me.

It was my grandmother's call at the foot of the stairs that brought me out of my slumber. "Time to get up or you'll be late for school! Happy birthday!" The dream seemed so real that my eyes still watered from the smell of the aftershave.

Though the dream had passed, the resolve stayed on. With the pure deductive reasoning learned from the Hardy Boys and Sherlock Holmes, it stood that in order for my voice to "crack," I first must say something. My mission therefore, was to take a birthday vow of silence. Mum's the word.

I don't suppose you have ever tried to make it through a day, particularly a school day, without talking. A Buddhist monk could no doubt do it standing on his head, but for a sixth-grader, the prospect was daunting. What was needed was a plan of action and, ponder as I might, no plan was forthcoming. The decision was made to wing it.

Pulling off this non-talking scheme at breakfast was a piece of cake. No cake really, breakfast was a bowl of cream of rice. The orange juice was from a big can kept in the refrigerator. An opener made little triangular holes in the top and what ended up in the glass at the breakfast table bore little resemblance to the picture on the label. Try as I might, the taste of Florida sunshine eluded me. The breakfast matched the gray morning skies.

Outside, a light snow fell, turning the green Studebaker into a big sugar cookie. Leaving for school, my grandmother's words through the kitchen door chilled me like a November morning. "The boy must be growing up. Did you notice how quiet he was?"

The snow sifted down through the old elms as my footsteps trod the "last mile" to the Blue Hill Consolidated School.

It was a morning made for pondering and, once again, Angel came into my thoughts. Ever since school had started in September, I sensed something was different about her. The way she had of popping into my head at awkward moments was becoming more and more unsettling.

Crossing the bridge at the Mill Brook and taking a moment to stand on the cement railing long enough to kick some snow into the rushing water beneath lifted my spirits slightly, but there was no getting away from the fact that not talking for a whole day of school was going to take some doing. One must understand that schools then were run on a different format than today. My teacher, though probably otherwise a wonderful person, ran the place with an iron hand. It was not uncommon for her to call on me at various times during class to ask my opinion regarding the answer to a problem in mathematics or, worse yet, spelling. She had an uncanny ability to ask only the questions that I could not answer. This particular teacher would expect an answer—though, with experience, she had come to expect the wrong answer.

The sidewalk took me past George Stevens Academy, Blue Hill's high school. It was logical that the guys in high school must be sporting cracked voices. Some of them even shaved daily, or so they claimed.

The consolidated school loomed ahead in the snow. Black smoke from the coal furnace wreathed about the place. The sign over the main entrance read, "Abandon all hope ye who enter here" or words to that effect, and a feeling of panic overtook me. How could I go all day without talking?

The front door seemed heavier than usual and echoed behind me with a slam. A wall of heat met my intrusion. The familiar school smell filled the inside air, a mixture of cafeteria food, chalk dust and that colored sawdust that the janitor used to clean the floors.

In panic mode, my only thought was to escape this oppression. A race down the hall into the playground was the work of a moment.

Once outside, my mind settled into the comfort of the familiar. I perused the playground. Angel was standing over by the slides. She looked in my direction, but shyness moved my eyes quickly to earth.

There were two slides put there for the enjoyment of the scholars, the big slide and the little slide. Though of different sizes, they both presented the same problem. On a wet or snowy morning, the first person down the slide would be doomed to spend the rest of the day with the seat of his pants soaking wet. No one wanted to go first. But, we had Wilmont. Wilmont had the distinction of being held back more that any other student in my tenure. However, what Wilmont lacked in scholastic abilities, he made up for in graciousness, and I suspect he didn't mind a wet trouser seat. There was a queue behind him as, like Sir Walter, he sacrificed his own so that others would be spared.

As if descending from Heaven, Angel was the fourth one down the slide. Something jumped inside my chest as she glided past and landed with a bump on the snow-covered ground.

The bell signaling the beginning of school picked that moment to ring. Lines formed according to grade, and we were marched in. Our line started to move slowly toward the door when I was aware of an impediment to my progress. It was Angel. She had hold of my arm and was leaning into my shoulder in the way that comes naturally to girls. There was no talking allowed in line, but her whisper roared into my ear. "Happy birthday, Sage."

The playground fluttered before my eyes and my knees turned to spaghetti. My sudden turning had the effect of causing her to brush against my cheek in a sort of accidental kiss. Forgetting my vow of silence, I attempted speech, my mouth opened and closed, but no actual words were forthcoming, only strange sounds. Sounds that one might hear uttered by a distressed mallard duck. My voice was cracked and broken.

As usual, Marnie was right.

Camp Nasty

The autumn sunshine had just melted the frost from the ferns lining the old track that would eventually lead to some acreage that needed my attention as a surveyor. The same sun, working on the resident air, stirred the dry oak leaves like a teaspoon in a bowl of cornflakes.

The oak leaves were not the only thing stirred by the breeze that morning. Memories, long buried by the sea of life, shifted their moorings and floated to the surface. Stepping beneath an ancient tree limb that had grown across the roadway, I stepped back in time.

About this time of year, my grandmother and grandfather would head to camp for a couple of weeks to "make wreaths." Conrad Rupert had a wreathing business and many of the households in town would make wreaths for so much a dozen. Conrad would supply the rings and wire, and the maker would provide the fir tips and the assembly. It provided Christmas money, but it ran to a good amount of work. Wreaths came in different sizes from the small 10-inch ring to the large 24-inch variety. They could be either single-faced or double-faced and, if not directed by demand, or Conrad, the maker had a choice according to preference. One thing that Conrad was particular about was that the wreaths be wound tight and that the fir brush be "round." Wreaths with flat brush were rejected. Some might call this a "cottage industry" but, in our case, it was a "camp" industry.

For those readers who did not grow up around here it may be necessary to explain exactly what a Maine "camp" is. First, a camp has nothing to do with tents. A camp is a building. Most families had a real house and a camp. The camp was used for an occasional get-away or retreat. Depending on their location, camps could be classified into two basic varieties—a camp on a pond or a hunting camp. It was always a tradition to open up a camp on the pond on Memorial Day. A hunting camp was more often used during November. Back then, a camp never had indoor plumbing, and only the fanciest had electricity.

Camp Nasty fell into the category of a hunting camp, though just to the west of it stood the remains of an old paddock, indicating that, in the distant past, horses were kept there for twitching wood.

The absence of running water and electric power was of no consequence to my grandparents. They were of the first generation since the beginning of mankind to experience these modern luxuries and then only during their adult lives.

My grandmother brought drinking water from home in glass gallon jugs. These jugs had a round finger hole at the neck. One had to be gentle with glass jugs and the pounding that they received in the back of the old pickup on the ride in over the woods road often lowered the number delivered from the number shipped.

There was a brook about a hundred yards from camp that provided water for other purposes. It was my job to lug two ten-quart pails full every morning up the path, back to camp.

Camp Nasty was not very large even by camp standards. To the left as you entered was a small wood stove with oven. Beside that was a cot that served as my sleeping quarters. Under a window, diagonally across from the stove, sat a table and chairs. At the very back was a double bed. Some cupboards rounded out the decorating scheme.

The place was as clean as a whistle and neat as a pin. The door was never locked and there was always some food left in the cupboard. It was understood that if a hunter stumbled onto the camp, he was welcome to build a fire to get warm, boil up some coffee, even make some biscuits. Many a time we would find a note of thanks pinned to the door. The note always had a name and the date of the visit. Game wardens were more formal; they left a printed card.

My grandfather, Bamp, had picked me up after school. He and my grandmother, Marnie, had gone out that morning to get the camp ready. By the time we got back to camp that Friday afternoon it was almost dark. The wood smoke from the metal stovepipe and a kerosene lamp in the window greeted our arrival. Marnie was cooking supper and the smell of vegetable soup (which always contained chunks of stew beef) mingled with the perfume of fir boughs Bamp had cut that afternoon.

Supper was early and so was bedtime. There was no television or radio to extend the evening. As was his custom, Bamp would hit the hay as soon as it was dark under the table.

The unfamiliar sounds of the forested night amplified the deepness of the silence. The window by my bed rattled with the chill November wind. Storm clouds raced before the moon and the forecast promised snow by morning. With Great-grandmother Cooper's quilt pulled tight under my chin, warmth settled over me like honey on a biscuit. Thoughts of tomorrow's adventures were quickly replaced by a dreamless sleep.

No prince in a palace could have wanted for more.

Thanksgiving Memories

Thanksgiving was a big deal in my family. The rules were set in stone and were followed assiduously year after year.

The first rule was that Thanksgiving dinner always took place at my grandparents' house. The whole darn family arrived around late morning and congregated in the kitchen. Grandmother would quickly tire of people being under foot and drive everyone out.

All the wives were expected to bring something to add to the meal. To this end, my grandmother was far too polite. She would invariably ask a daughter-in-law, "Dear, could you bring your French-cut string bean and onion ring casserole? Everyone enjoys it so."

"Oh, certainly, you mean the one made with Campbell's cream of mushroom soup? And should I also make that lime Jello and Cool Whip dessert?"

"Yes, dear, that is always a big hit."

The second rule was that dinner, in the true Maine tradition, was always the noon meal, but usually it was mid-afternoon before we all sat down.

The dining table was cobbled together from three or four smaller tables and was always beautifully set. Tablecloths that hadn't seen the light of day since last year's Thanksgiving were pressed into service. These tablecloths were all old, and most displayed a level of handwork and needlework that set them apart. Each tablecloth had a story. "Now, this one was given to Mother Cooper when she was first married and setting up housekeeping in the old Smith place on Beech Hill."

Serving dishes, too, had stories of their own. "This is Grammy Billings' berry bowl. She was very choice of it."

Depending on the number of cousins available, there was at least one children's table, sometimes two or three. Children's tables were separated, by distance and sometimes doors, from the main table. It is unclear how one ascended to the main table. It could have been age, except that my uncle Burke, well after he had reached man's estate, would sometimes join us at the children's table. It seems the children's table was always more fun.

At Thanksgiving, girl cousins were in the majority. As a matter of fact, for the first ten or so years of my life, the delegation of boy cousins consisted entirely of me. By way of wanting a son, my uncle Jimmie had six daughters, the oldest three being my yearly companions at the children's table.

It wasn't as if we children were second rate, but Grandmother was a practical woman. We did not use the good china, for instance. Our water glasses were not crystal and the serving dishes on our table were not priceless heirlooms. The tablecloth was very pretty but, being of some plastic material, was not prone to stains.

About 2:30 in the afternoon Grandmother would call the meeting to order. Everyone would take their place. As grace was being said even the children would sit quietly.

Then, Uncle Jimmie would carve the turkey. Carving a turkey is an art, and he was master of his craft. Sometimes the seating was such that a boy could watch and learn the correct way. The steel against the blade, the initial cut and the subsequent cuts. Effortless then, impossible for me now.

Often it would snow and the sight of the flakes through the old glass of the windows, mixing with the aromas of wood smoke from the stove and pumpkin pie from the oven, would give even a 10-year-old boy pause to be thankful.

I see Uncle Oscar has the checkerboard set up and it is time for me to get out Grammy Billings' berry bowl which now resides in my sideboard. Happy Thanksgiving!

O, Christmas Tree

It was an excited boy of 9 who waited impatiently by the kitchen door that Saturday morning. His faithful dog Pup shared in the excitement, though Pup had no idea what the excitement was about. To Pup it didn't matter. He got excited about everything. Dogs are like that.

Boy and dog shared a common exuberance coupled to a wonderment as to why it took adults so long to do things. Golly, there was a Christmas tree to get and we were burning daylight just waiting.

The day was on the mild side with a meager cover of wet snow. Not exactly the best weather for the annual Christmas tree hunt, but it would have to do. This was a very special event, at least to me. Others seemed to look on it as more of a chore. Perhaps adults lost some of the Christmas spirit over time or perhaps children absorbed it so greedily that there was not any left over for grownups. My belief is that the former rather than the latter is the case. The Christmas spirit is like love. There is plenty of it to go around. It's just a question of one taking advantage of it.

The thing about standing around the warm indoors when dressed for the cold outdoors is that the body starts to overheat, particularly in the area of the feet. For reasons unexplained, rubber packs were the winter boot of choice. Looking back, it was clear that they were of no earthly good. When new, and a size over, enough woolen socks could be inserted to keep the feet fairly warm and dry. However, packs were a once-a-year purchase and tended to show up under the Christmas tree. At the time of this story, nearly a year had passed since the boots were new. My feet had grown two sizes and the boots were covered with colorful glued-on rubber patches. These patches were to plug the many holes and to keep the water out. It is a scientific fact that these patches never, ever, ever worked.

By and by the Christmas tree hunt was officially begun. A splitting ax was discovered by the wood pile and we were off.

The old Stover farm had over 200 acres on the west side of the road and 25 more on the east side. More than ample land to find a Christmas tree, or so one would assume.

We walked down the field road to the spot where it crossed the brook. The brook was small and happy. It ran free most of the year except in the driest summer. That day the brook, though covered with ice, could be seen babbling beneath the shroud of crystal that it wore during the winter months. Pup scampered across the surface. Pup was a guide for me when crossing questionable ice. If he ventured out, it was safe for me to follow. Such was the logic of a 9-year-old boy. Again, Pup was right. The ice held and we continued through the upper field.

At the head of that field was a tree that looked like it would fill the bill. It was rejected by the ax carrier and the party continued into the upper pasture. The pasture was called that because it had once been fenced off for sheep to browse. That was well before my time and large trees bowed down over the woods road, forming a darkened tunnel that added to the dimness of an already overcast December day.

It seemed as though we walked over the whole 200 acres. More and more trees were sighted. Each, in turn, was rejected for one reason or another. Nature's trees are never perfect when viewed with a critical eye.

It was close to 3:30 and daylight was waning as we walked out of the woods into the upper field.

The first tree we had spotted was silhouetted by the last rays of sun.

The remark was made that this was the perfect tree. "How had we walked past and missed it?"

A rhetorical question that remains unanswered.

List of Illustrations

A selection of other titles available from Penobscot Books

Visit penbaypress.me for full descriptions
of these and other books we offer.

Island Naturalist — 2015 Maine Literary Awards Winner
by Kathie Fiveash $27.95

Floating Palaces—America's Queens of the Sea
(Maine Island Mariners and the Big Steam Yachts)
by William A. Haviland and Barbara L. Britton $33.95

GOTCHA! April Fool!
(Stories published in Penobscot Bay Press newspapers
1964-2012)
by Jerry Durnbaugh, Nat Barrows, Hugh Bowden
and David Walsh $25.95

An Island Sense of Home: Stories from Isle au Haut
by Harold S. van Doren $37.95

I Loved This Work....I have been delightfully busy
by John T. Crowell with accompanying DVD $49.95

The Best of K's Kwisine
by Harry Kaiserian $39.95

Order online at penbaypress.me or call 207-374-2341.

Penobscot Books

A division of Penobscot Bay Press
P.O. Box 36, 69 Main St. Stonington ME 04681
books@pbp.me • penbaypress.me
207-367-2200